D1266407

THE ROYAL HOMES & GARDENS

Buckingham Palace Gardens

Windsor Castle

Castle of Mey

The Royal Trains

Birkhall

THE ROYAL HOMES & GARDENS

a private view

by Douglas Sutherland & Anthony Purdy

Leslie Frewin Publishers Limited

First published in 1966 by:
Leslie Frewin Publishers Limited
15 Hay's Mews, London W.1

Copyright 1966 by:
Douglas Sutherland and
Anthony Purdy

Designed by: M. Mohan

Printed by Anchor Press and
bound by William Brendon,
both of Tiptree, Essex

Contents

Introduction

The manner in which our Royal Family live is a matter of perennial interest to us all. Most of us like to think of them, not as remote figures living a life of unimaginable splendour, but as a family with the same sort of problems as our own, even if the circumstances of their daily life are vastly different.

This book does not set out to describe the intimate home life of the Queen and her immediate family but, because it is about the official and private residences in which they live, it is hoped that it will give an insight into some of the special problems of being the First Family in the land. A home, whether it be a palace or a cottage, reflects the personality of the people who live in it more surely than anything else. The Queen's residences are no exception.

There is, too, another side to the coin. It is not unusual nowadays to hear criticism of the style in which the Royal residences are maintained. It has become a hardy annual in Parliamentary debates and a whipping boy for certain politicians who pretend not to understand why three official residences are required to carry out the Royal function. It is interesting, in this connection, to recollect that Queen Elizabeth I required fourteen palaces in regular use to support her monarchy and Henry VIII before her had well over twenty.

Again, this book does not set out to enter the political lists but to describe the function of each of the Royal residences – the official role of Buckingham Palace and the historical significance of Windsor Castle and Holyroodhouse, as well as the value to the Royal Family of their private homes like Balmoral and Sandringham.

Gardens, no less than homes, reflect the personality of their owners. It was Kipling who wrote: 'The Glory of the Garden lies in more than meets the eye'.

It is hoped that this account of the Royal homes and their gardens will convey to the reader more than meets the eye, for the glory and traditions of our British monarchy are both real and intangible. It is the aim of this book to make some of the intangible more real.

THE AUTHORS

Buckingham House, built in 1703. George III
bought it in 1762

Buckingham Palace

Buckingham Palace is the official residence of the Queen in London and the best known Royal residence in the world.

It stands on a site once occupied by Buckingham House which was built in 1705 by John Sheffield, Duke of Buckingham. It suited the Duke's purpose admirably for it was close to the seat of the Government at Westminster and conveniently near the City of London – yet it had the advantages of a country estate. The Berkeley hunt used to meet where Charing Cross now stands and he could shoot wild fowl in the marshy land which bordered the Thames.

Down the years, the official residence of the Monarch had been in turn the Palaces of Westminster, Whitehall and St James's. When Buckingham House was acquired by George III in 1762, it was bought on a whim as the town house for his wife Queen Charlotte. The price he paid for the house and the surrounding lands was £28,000 which must rate as a considerable bargain. Today the value of the site together with the forty-two acres of private grounds in which it stands is inestimable.

It was George IV who decided to make the old Buckingham House into his official London home. For this purpose he obtained a grant of public money from Parliament to enlarge the existing building and decorate it in a style suitable for State occasions. The limitations imposed on him by Parliament did not, however, appeal to him. Instead of building on to the existing structure, he pulled the whole thing down and started again.

Fortunately George was a man capable of appreciating the virtues of good architecture. He appointed his close friend Nash to design the new building. Nash was, of course, the outstanding architect of his age. He had already created his superb terraces around Regent's Park and designed the Regent Street quadrant but, when he started work on Buckingham Palace in 1821, he was already nearing the end of his working life. It was not fully completed when he died in 1835.

What Nash left behind was an elegantly proportioned house built around three sides of a square with the east side left open. On that side, which looks down the Mall, he created a magnificently ornate gateway which became known as the Marble Arch.

The choice of the architect Blore to carry on where Nash left off was not nearly such a happy one. Blore proceeded to close in the open east side with a new wing which effectively concealed most of Nash's original design and, in 1847, the Marble Arch was moved to where it now stands on the old site of the Tyburn gallows.

George did not survive to live in the Palace which he had created and his

Buckingham Palace from the air

GROUND FLOOR

1 Palace Superintendent's Flat 2 Housekeeper's Flat 3 Records 4 Keeper of Privy Purse 5 Doctor's Surgery 6 Treasurer 7 Files 8 Clerk and Typists 9 Royal Family Stairs 10 Queen's Private Secretary 11 Footmen's Room 12 Assistant Private Secretary 13 Equerry 14 Assistant Private Secretary 15 Press Secretary 16 Duke's Treasurer 17 Duke's Secretary 18 Queen's Lift 19 Swimming Pool 20 Belgian Suite 21 1844 Room 22 Reception 23 Bow Room 24 Grand Hall 25 Household Dining Room 26 Service 27 Queen's Cinema 28 Art Gallery 29 Kitchen and Stores 30 Corridor to Grand Hall 31 Police 32 Guard Room 33 Post Office 34 Pay Office

FIRST FLOOR

35 Balcony Room 36–39 Buhl Room Suite 40 Chinese Dining Room 41 Pine Room 42 Prince Philip's Audience Room 43 Prince Philip's Suite 44 Prince Philip's Page 45 Prince Philip's Dressing Room 46–47 Prince Philip's Bathroom 48 Queen's Dressing Room 49 Queen's Bedroom 50 Queen's Sitting Room 51 Queen's Dining Room 52 Spare Room 53 Spare Room 54 Queen's Audience Room 55 Queen's Lift 56 Ante-room 57 Royal Closet 58 Throne Room 59 White Drawing Room 60 Music Room 61 Stairs 62 Green Drawing Room 63 State Dining Room 64 Blue Room 65 Ante-room 66 Ballroom 67 Staff Dining Room 68 Three Spare Bedrooms 69 Three Spare Bedrooms 70 Master of Household 71–73 Clerks 74–77 State Guest Suite

SECOND FLOOR

78–83 Rooms for Ladies-in-Waiting 84 School and Music Room 85–86 Princess Anne's Rooms 87 Prince Charles' Room 88 Princess Anne's and Prince Charles' Sitting Room 89 Spare Room 90 Day Nursery 91 Prince Charles' Bathroom 92 Prince Edward's Night Nursery 93 Prince Andrew's Room 94 Governess's Room 95 School 96 Sitting Room 97 Spare Room 98 Wardrobe 99–100 Rooms for Queen's Dresser 101–103 Rooms for Valets 104 Queen's Wardrobe 105–106 Store Rooms 107–111 Maids' Rooms 112 State Apartments 113 Staff Rooms 114 Maids' Quarters

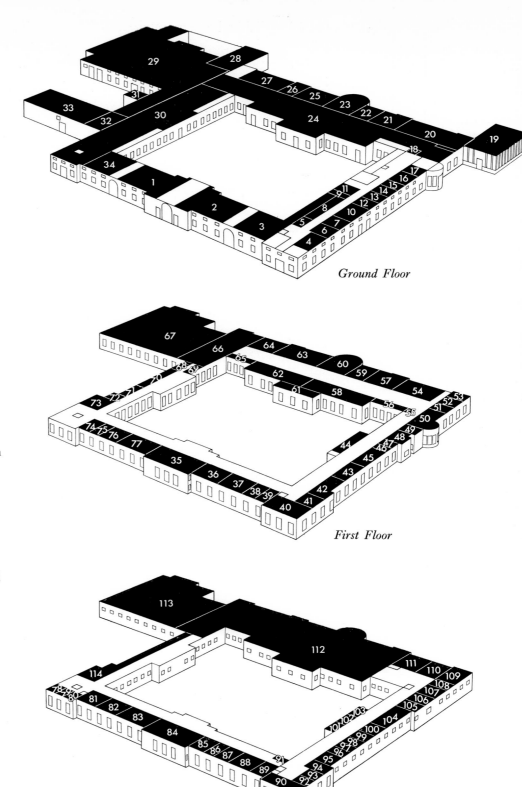

Ground Floor

First Floor

Second Floor

brother William who succeeded him disliked it so much that he tried to sell it. It was Queen Victoria who surprised everyone by moving there from St James's Palace soon after her accession. She never disguised the fact, however, that she also did not really like it as a home. The endless corridors made it a cold and impersonal house. At the same time she complained that it was 'too small'. After the death of Prince Albert, she seldom went there except for State functions and spent a great deal of her widowhood at Osborne. Oddly enough, although Buckingham Palace had now become the centre of Court life, foreign ambassadors continued to be accredited to the Court of St James's – as they do to this day.

It was not until George V came to the throne that anything further was done to bring the Palace up-to-date. In 1913 he had the east façade re-designed by Sir Aston Webb. At the same time, Webb designed the fountains and the statue to Queen Victoria which stand outside the gates and built Admiralty Arch at the other end of the Mall. It is this aspect, so vastly changed from the original conception by Nash, which has become so well known. Of the old Buckingham House, only the Royal Mews built by George III remain. He also had the State coach built which is housed there and which has been used for Coronations ever since.

It is probably true to say that the only Royal tenant of Buckingham Palace who actually enjoyed living there was Queen Mary, who took a more than usually close interest in the running of the Palace and in rearranging its fabulous art treasures so that they showed up to the best advantage. Certainly it is an unwieldy and uneconomic proposition with its 600 rooms and half a mile of corridors. It takes a corps of over 100 cleaners to keep its largely unused rooms dusted and a staff of a further 100, from Court officials to minor servants, to maintain it as the operational headquarters in London of the Royal Family.

Buckingham Palace is, however, a completely necessary adjunct to the efficient working of the Monarchy. It is the place where most of the important heads of visiting States are accommodated as well as fulfilling a multiplicity of domestic roles from the holding of the annual Garden Parties for up to ten thousand people to the giving of the small and intimate luncheons which is the way in which the Queen and Prince Philip like to keep themselves in touch with the views of their subjects.

The interior of Buckingham Palace has only changed in points of minor detail over the last hundred years. The main pattern of the Palace has remained exactly the same and indeed it is hard to see how any major alterations could be made to the formalised lay-out of the great State apartments and the ornately furnished corridors. The corridors are an important feature of the interior of the house and have the appearance of beautifully decorated ante-rooms. In the west wing, which overlooks the private gardens, the State Apartments open off either side of a broad corridor which is over twenty feet wide. On the ground floor it is known as the Marble Corridor and, on the

The Principal Corridor in Buckingham Palace Royal Apartments

first floor, it serves the purpose of a picture gallery where many of the unique collection of Dutch paintings collected by George IV are hung. On the other three sides of the quadrangle, the corridors only give entrance to rooms on one side and look onto the courtyard on the other. The most important one, known as the Principal Corridor, runs behind the east wing and gives access to the Balcony Room from which the Royal Family make their appearances in the front of the Palace, and to the suites given to the accommodation of Royal Guests.

The State Apartments are all in the west wing. On the ground floor are the rooms most familiar to visitors to the Palace – the Grand Entrance and the Grand Hall where receptions are sometimes held. Beyond these, on the other side of the Marble Corridor, are the Household Dining Room and the smaller reception rooms like the famous Bow Room, the 1844 Room where the intimate Palace lunch parties are held and the Belgian Suite where Prince Andrew and Prince Edward were born. These rooms have changed little with successive generations but a modern note is struck at either end of the west wing. At one end is an apartment which has been converted into a cinema for the Queen's use and at the other end a swimming pool has been built onto the end of the wing.

For the most part the remainder of the ground floor is devoted to the many offices engaged in running the Palace. The Keeper of the Privy Purse who looks after the Queen's private affairs has his office there; so do the Private Secretary, the Duke's Secretary and Treasurer, the Queen's Equerry and the Palace Doctor. There are rooms for the Royal Housekeeper, the Palace Superintendent and the Palace Guard. There is a pay office, a filing room and a records room. There is even a police room and a post office.

The important State Apartments are on the first floor. There is the State Dining Room, hung around with portraits of former Monarchs and lit by magnificent chandeliers, as are all the great State Apartments. The dining room table is over eight feet across and, when it is fully expanded, is eighty-one feet long – fifteen feet longer than a cricket pitch. On this floor, too, are the great ballroom, little changed from the days when Queen Victoria's guests arrived there to waltz in their crinolines, the bow-fronted Music Room and the Blue Room. The north end of the west wing is devoted to State Apartments used for more personal Royal occasions. There is the Queen's Audience Room and the White Drawing Room where many of the Royal christening parties and wedding receptions are held. In each corner of the White Drawing Room stand identical ebony china cabinets. One, however, is different. It conceals a secret door through which the members of the Royal Family can escape to a small withdrawing room. By pressing a hidden spring, the cabinet and the mirror above it swing back to give access to this private room where they can rest during a reception before rejoining the crowded State Apartments.

The private apartments of the Queen and the Duke are on the second

Grand Entrance Hall of Buckingham Palace

A rare photograph of Edward VII's ante-room
adjoining his study in Buckingham Palace. There
are nineteen hats and a large collection of umbrellas

The Empress of Russia's suite, Buckingham Palace.
This room is today a principal bedroom for State
visitors. The photograph was taken about 1900

Above:
The Palace Throne Room

Right:
Part of the Throne Room ceiling at the Palace

The Green Room of the Palace. The doorway leads
to the White Room

floor and take up most of the north wing. The Royal Bedroom is a fine room, simply but comfortably furnished and with a big bow-fronted window which gives it a spacious air. It is flanked on one side by a small sitting room and on the other by the Queen's dressing room. Beyond this is a bathroom, Prince Philip's dressing room and his private study which opens into another small audience room.

The second floor of the Palace is almost entirely devoted to bedroom accommodation for the large number of staff who 'live in', for the ladies-in-waiting and, most important of all, for the Royal children. It was in the reign of George VI that the children's suite first came into being. A group of five rooms was set aside for the young Princesses which were later to become the first married home of the present Queen and Prince Philip before they moved to Clarence House. In the present reign, the space allotted to the children has been added to so that with school rooms and other adjuncts they now occupy most of the east and north wings.

As with all the private apartments in the Palace, the children's quarters strike a much less formal note so that they are more the sort of rooms one would expect to find in a private home. The Queen and Prince Philip themselves prefer to work in a homely atmosphere and surround themselves in their suite with favourite photographs and possessions. Prince Philip's study in particular shows the stamp of his personality. Although it is conventionally furnished, there are modern gadgets everywhere like dictaphones and tape recorders which testify to his up-to-date outlook. There is the same personalisation in the sitting room which Prince Charles and Princess Anne share and in the day and night nurseries of the younger children. All around them they have their private trophies and they are allowed to say what style they want in the furnishing and decorating of their own rooms. This informality is carried through into the way they live, and, although the menus are still written in French, the food is less pretentious than might be found in many private homes. In the winter there are open fires and the general air is more that of a comfortable country house than an official Royal residence in the centre of London.

Just the same, Buckingham Palace is still a house with an inescapably official atmosphere. In spite of the many labour-saving devices which have been introduced – mainly at the instigation of Prince Philip – it is still a house which needs a staff of almost two hundred to keep it in running order and enable it to function efficiently as the place from which the Queen carries out most of her constitutional duties. It is true that the old-fashioned and unworkable heating system has been replaced in recent years with an up-to-date oil-fired system. It is true, too, that the working arrangements of the Royal Household have been greatly streamlined. There is a nice story that Queen Victoria once asked the Master of the Household to see that a fire was lit in her dining room only to be told that it was not his business. It was up to the Lord Steward to order it to be laid and up to the Lord

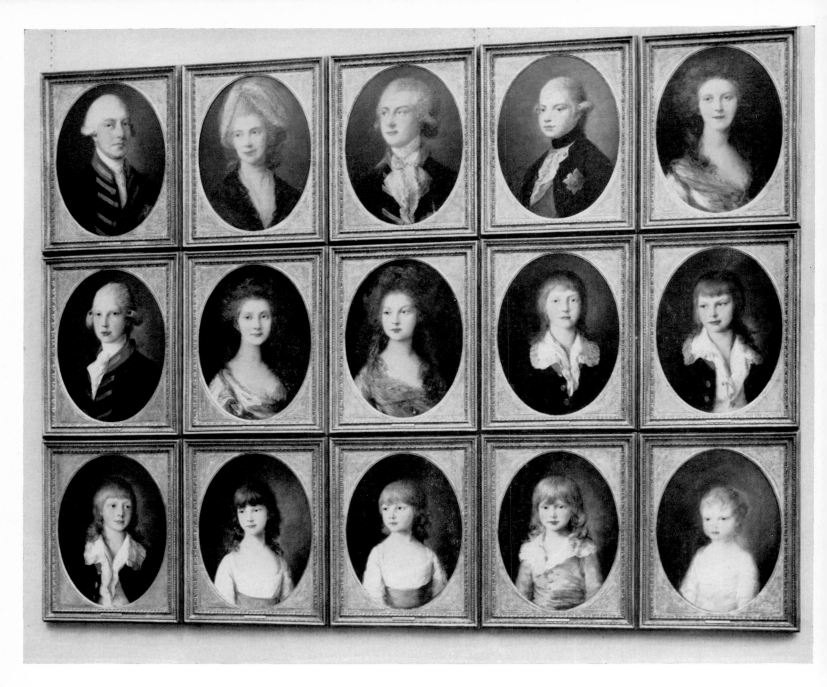

Gainsborough's portraits of the family of George III and Queen Charlotte. They were painted at Windsor in the Autumn of 1782

Buckingham Palace: the White Drawing Room

A corner of the White
Drawing Room, Buckingham
Palace, showing a unique
door in the form of a mirror,
leading to the Royal Closet

Chamberlain to see that it was lit! That is all changed now. Just the same a request from the Queen for a cup of tea is still apt to set off a chain reaction and involve a series of functionaries before it can be complied with.

The day to day running of the Palace is a mixture of the commonplace and the extraordinary. At first light each morning a small army of daily women arrive to help with the dusting and cleaning. After them the earliest caller is the newspaper boy who delivers the magazines and papers at the Privy Purse's Office at 7 am. He is followed half an hour later by the post van which brings the Royal mail in locked and sealed boxes. Bread is delivered daily in an ordinary Lyons van and the garbage is collected twice a week. It also requires a twice weekly visit from an oil tanker to keep the heating system in operation.

It is the very magnitude of the task of keeping the Palace going which makes it out of the ordinary. The laundry bill comes to £100 a week and the cost of the telephone service with its 250 extensions comes to about £8,000 a year. During the last century the extravagance of the Palace was a byword. Lighting was by candles which were never allowed to be lit twice so that the 'Palace ends' as they were known were a valuable perquisite for the servants. The story is often told that, when Prince Philip started to enquire into the economics of the Household, he discovered that thousands of candles were still being ordered every month in spite of the fact that electricity had long ago been installed.

Critics of the Royal Family are quick to point out that the cost of maintaining the Palace is a heavy drain on public money but this is not strictly true. Although Buckingham Palace is an official residence and as such becomes a charge on the Ministry of Works, this only applies in so far as the actual upkeep of the structure is concerned. All the entertainment of the many thousands of guests every year and the actual day to day running costs are the financial responsibility of the Queen personally who pays for it out of the Privy Purse. It is interesting to note that she gets £5,000 a year less for this purpose than did George V, in spite of the very considerable increase in the cost of living.

The Palace gardens

Buckingham Palace – Gardens

When George IV commissioned Nash to design his new Palace he also employed the great landscape gardener, W. T. Aiton, to lay out the grounds. The result was an overall scheme which has stood the test of time as being both practical and beautiful.

Perhaps the thing which first strikes one when viewing the Buckingham Palace gardens is their simplicity. There is the minimum of 'fussiness'. Where there are flower beds they are laid out on a splendid scale, the sweep of lawn is impressive and the many rare trees are carefully sited so that they can be seen to their best advantage.

The lawn extends from the terrace behind the west wing and is frequently used in the summer for the garden parties which are such a feature of the Royal year. It also is required to serve as a landing pad for Prince Philip's helicopter – a function which can scarcely have been foreseen by the industrious Mr Aiton! Much of the lawn is of camomile. The advantage of camomile is, of course, that it remains a brilliant green all the year round and survives even the longest periods of drought. It is generally believed that the camomile was specially introduced but this is not so. It appeared by accident and George V liked it so much that he encouraged it to spread with the result that it now predominates.

In general effect the gardens to the west of the Palace resemble the layout of the Green Park gardens – an impression which is accentuated by the artificial lake which has been created amongst the trees at the Birdcage Walk end. Designed in the rough shape of the letter S, it extends to some four acres and is the home for a surprising variety of bird life. Many types of duck and even wild geese nest around its sides and on the little island in the middle. Oddly enough there were no fish in the lake until, during the last war, a bomb fell into the Serpentine in Hyde Park and damaged the grid which covered the entrance to the underground stream by which the Royal lake got its water supply. Some of the Serpentine fish took advantage of the incident to escape down the tunnel so that the Royal lake now has a healthy population of chub, roach and perch.

The little island which can be reached by a punt was a never ending source of delight to the Queen and Princess Margaret when they were children. It was the scene of many exciting games of make believe and an ideal place for picnics and having Girl Guide camps. Two years ago, the Queen made it even more exciting for her children by having a waterfall constructed at one end of the lake. When the lake was first dug, the soil which was excavated was used to create a high bank which blanks off the Royal Mews and which in spring is a mass of daffodils. Beyond that are the Royal greenhouses which house many exotic plants.

Above:
The four-acre lake is an attractive feature of the
Buckingham Palace garden

Right:
Princes Andrew and Edward in Buckingham Palace
garden

The lake – probably the most rural scene in
London

Buckingham Palace: another view of the lake

The Royal Family still
maintain a fleet of carriages
for State occasions

taken place. During Queen Victoria's long reign, many laurel bushes and other dull evergreens so beloved by the Victorians had been allowed to flourish. George V, who disliked change, allowed them to remain but his son who was an extremely keen and talented gardener, made a determined effort to replace them with more colourful shrubs. It is a policy which has been followed ever since and resulted in the opening up of new vistas of beauty.

By contrast, modern times have brought their own problems which have forced a different approach on the Royal gardeners. With London developing upwards, it was inevitable that the total privacy of the gardens would be destroyed by skyscraper buildings, commanding an eagle's eye view. To counteract this there is a tree planting scheme in progress but it will be many years before the Royal Family will be able to use their gardens as freely as they have been used to. Just the same, the grounds and gardens of Buckingham Palace and the facilities they offer for relaxation are greatly prized by the Queen and Prince Philip – and perhaps even more so by the Royal children.

The children have their own corner set aside for them. At a point where the Queen herself can keep an eye on them from the desk where she works, there is a sandpit and a climbing frame and even a miniature caravan where they can play at houses. The summer house is again in use for lessons and another generation of Royal children are enjoying the delights of the lake and the island.

We should not leave Buckingham Palace without mention of the Royal Mews. These are contained by the south wall of the Palace grounds and may be visited by the public between the hours of 2 pm and 4 pm every Wednesday and Thursday throughout the year. They are well worth a visit both from an architectural point of view as well as to see the Queen's horses and the splendid display of coaches and carriages including the State coaches.

An unusual view of the
Palace: the rear

Windsor: the gardens of the Royal Apartments

Windsor Castle

Few houses, viewed from a distance, can have a more dramatic profile than Windsor Castle. Silhouetted against the skyline it is everybody's idea of what a mediæval stronghold should look like and it is, in fact, the oldest Royal residence in the world. It has been the home of the kings and queens of England for over eight hundred years and even before that the site was a fortified stronghold created by William the Conqueror. Henry I was the first king who actually lived there but today the earliest identifiable stonework dates from the reign of Henry II (1154–89). This ancient part of the Castle is now part of the Royal Apartments next to the East Terrace.

The luckless King John was actually besieged in Windsor by his own Barons in 1189 and it was from Windsor in 1215 that he made the two-mile journey to Runnymede to sign the Magna Carta.

To view Windsor at closer quarters, however, is to be struck with its air of newness so that it takes on the rather spurious appearance of a film set. This at first disappointing effect is in large measure due to the work of restoration carried out by Sir Jeffry Wyatville in the early 1800's. He imposed the then fashionable Gothic look on much of the old structure which conceals many interesting features. A 'modernisation' can also be seen which was carried out by the French architect Slavin, on the Curfew Tower which dates from 1227. He had it completely refaced and crowned with a pointed roof in the style favoured by the castle builders of his own land. The interior of the Castle, however, leaves nothing to be desired in the evidence of its antiquity. Some of the ancient and original masonry of the Curfew Tower, for example, can still be seen. At one point in the same tower there is the beginning of a tunnel dug by a long-forgotten prisoner in his efforts to escape and the Tower also houses a pair of stocks in excellent working order!

One of the Royal tenants who left his indelible mark on the Castle was Edward III. He was born there and it was Edward who founded the historic Order of the Garter of Windsor. The origin of the Garter is said to stem from an incident which occurred when Edward was walking in the grounds of Windsor with the members of his Court. The Countess of Salisbury lost one of her garters and the king retrieved it. Some of the nobles standing by started to snigger whereupon Edward turned to them and said, 'Sirs, the time shall shortlie come when yee shall attribute much honour unto such a garter'. He made it the symbol of a new order of chivalry, attaching to it the famous motto *Honi soit qui mal y pense*. When St George's Chapel was completed in 1528, it became the spiritual home of the order as it has remained to the present day. The St George's Day procession of the sovereign and the knights wearing their Garter robes remains one of the most colourful

An aerial view of Windsor Castle showing the
East Terrace gardens and orangery right

St George's Chapel, Windsor

The State Apartments, Windsor

of the ancient ceremonies whilst the magnificent architecture of the Chapel itself makes it one of our most valued heritages.

Apart from founding the Order of the Garter, Edward III also undertook a great deal of building at Windsor which included the Canon's Cloister which can still be seen in its original form. It was not, however, for another hundred years that much more was done to the Castle. When the boy King Edward IV inherited it, it was still very much a fortress with few refinements as a Royal residence. 'Methinks I am in a prison,' he complained. 'Here be no galleries nor no gardens to walk in.' It was he who built the Horseshoe Cloister in the shape of one of his own badges, a fetlock. Its purpose was to give accommodation for the clergy from the fine church he had built nearby. In the tradition of the times there were many houses clustering round and abutting on the Castle walls which had been built for the convenience of courtiers and clergy and which were pulled down or reconstructed from time to time to make room for other building projects. The Horseshoe Cloister has however remained as a permanent home for church officials.

Windsor continued to play its part down the years of history but it was not until a woman, Elizabeth I, came to the throne that it started to become less of a fortress and more of a home. She constructed the magnificent

Holbein, Van Dyke, Canaletto, Windsor is an art gallery of Old Masters. Many rooms, such as this, have exquisite murals on walls and ceilings

A drawing room at Windsor

North Terrace with its fine views over the Home Park and the Buckinghamshire hills beyond. She intended it as a place where she could take exercise and enjoy the view during wet weather. It is now used to house the Royal Library.

The Castle became a prison again when it played its part in the tragedy of Charles I. He was confined there for a short time before his execution and it was to the Deanery of St George's that his faithful friends brought his body back for burial. He lies in a vault beneath the choir close to the Albert Memorial Chapel which is the present resting place of our kings and queens.

After the restoration Charles II was the first Monarch who really concerned himself with the outside of the Castle – an aspect of living at Windsor which greatly appeals to our present Royal Family. Charles enjoyed the stag hunting in the Great Park and he had the magnificent avenue of elms planted to form the Long Walk on the south side. The elms survived until 1945 when disease caused them to be cut down. George VI had them replaced with an avenue of chestnut and plane trees. Charles II loved the grandeur of Windsor and, it is said, vied with Louis XIV to create a home which could match Versailles in magnificence. He built much of what are the present State Apartments and commissioned the Italian Verrio to paint the ceilings and Grinling Gibbons to carve the woodwork. Much of Verrio's work has since crumbled but a wealth of Gibbons' carvings remain and the whole rich interior makes a fine setting for a collection of some of the most valuable of the Royal pictures.

When Charles had first occupied Windsor it was after it had been invested by Cromwell's soldiers and they had left it in a sorry state having looted many of its treasures. By the time he died it had been restored to far greater glory and it was a favourite retreat for Queen Anne who was also devoted to outdoor pursuits. She followed the Royal buckhounds and started the tradition of the Ascot Races. Dean Swift records having seen her 'driving furiously like Jehu . . . a mighty hunter like Nimrod' – sometimes covering forty miles in an afternoon. She also bought what became known as the Queen's Lodge opposite the Castle in the Home Park and this became her favourite retreat when illness and her increasing weight made her sporting activities impractical.

The Hanoverians who followed Anne were, however, of a different mind about Windsor. George I and II positively disliked the place and during their reigns it was shamefully neglected. It became a rabbit warren of grace and favour houses and apartments and was divided up into so many parts that its interior took on the appearance of a tenement. George III regarded it more highly but on the whole preferred to live at Queen's Lodge while the local lads used the Castle as a playground.

It was left to George IV to bring the situation again under control. He was an enthusiastic house builder. Alongside his grandiose plans for Buckingham Palace, he got a grant of £150,000 from Parliament to improve Windsor.

As in the case of Buckingham Palace, it did not prove nearly enough. It was he who commissioned Sir Jeffry Wyatville to create a worthy Palace within the walls of the ancient fortress and the gratified architect set to with a will. By the time he had finished he had spent almost a million pounds and had created the look of 'newness' which has already been commented on. Perhaps his most important contribution to the interior was the building of the Grand Corridor which runs round two sides of the quadrangle and is 550 feet long. He also created the memorial Waterloo Chamber. It is an ornate room, impressive for its size more than anything else. The floor is covered with one of the largest seamless carpets in existence, eighty feet by forty, and the dining room table is large enough to accommodate 150 guests at one sitting.

In many ways George IV was the creator of modern Windsor. He banished the crowds who had been accustomed to come every Sunday to hear the band play and peer through the windows, and closed the Home Park to visitors. In altering the Long Walk so that it came right up to the Castle gates he had Queen's Lodge pulled down but, although he made Windsor once again a Royal residence, he did little to make it a comfortable place for his courtiers. Even by Queen Victoria's day attending Courts at Windsor were viewed with mixed feelings. She selected Wyatville's Grand Corridor as a suitable place to hold her audiences. Visitors awaiting their turn to be received were forced to hang around, sometimes for hours, in this vast draughty cavern before being called forward to the Queen's presence.

Prince Albert in particular was fond of Windsor. Sandringham had not yet been purchased by the Royal Family and so the Castle was much in use as a country house to which they could retreat from the formality of the life at Buckingham Palace. He went there as often as he could and eventually he died there. To the end of her own life Queen Victoria preserved the room in which he died exactly as it had been in his lifetime even to the extent of the bottle of medicine by the bedside and having the water on the washstand changed every day. Although visits to Windsor had lost much of their savour after the death of her Consort, she continued to go there frequently and became known as the Widow of Windsor.

Edward VII bought Sandringham while he was still Prince of Wales and it had a high place in his affections principally because he was able to indulge his favourite sport of pheasant shooting there. He used Windsor almost only at Easter and during Ascot week and it was not used a great deal more often during the reign of his successor George V. The infrequency of their visits, however, did not deter Queen Mary from taking a great interest in the Castle. She had a wonderful genius for home making and she did much to improve the private apartments, making them much less stiffly formal and displaying the treasures with which they are filled to the best advantage.

The private apartments are contained in the south and east wings and look out over formal gardens laid out round a central fountain. Immaculately pruned shrubs alternate with statues and symmetrical rose beds provide

The white drawing room, showing the magnificent french cabinet by Gouthière brilliant splashes of colour. The whole of the formal garden is enclosed by the East Terrace and beneath the terrace walk there is a delightful, old-fashioned orangery, which now contains a swimming-bath.

There can be no mention of Queen Mary in connection with Windsor, however, without bringing Frogmore into the story. The Frogmore property first became a Royal property in the reign of Henry VIII and in Queen Elizabeth's time Shakespeare made it the setting for one of the scenes of *The Merry Wives of Windsor*. It was the practice in those days, however, for it to be let and it was not until George III's day when his Queen Charlotte went to live there that it became a Royal residence. Charlotte had her Vice-Chamberlain, William Price, lay out the gardens. He dammed the narrow stream and drained the surrounding land to form what is now known as the Canal and used the rich soil excavated from the river bed to construct artificial banks to relieve the flatness of the surroundings. They remain one of the most attractive features of the present-day gardens.

Queen Victoria also loved Frogmore. She cleared much of the ground and planted it with flowering trees and shrubs and laid out spacious lawns. It was Queen Mary, however, who turned the gardens into some of the most beautiful in Britain. She had planted there all manner of rare and beautiful things. Her interest in Frogmore grew out of the time when she had lived there as Princess of Wales. The late King and Queen Elizabeth also lived there as Duke and Duchess of York, so it has many happy memories for the present Royal Family as a private and restful retreat. It was George VI who first gave permission for the public to visit the gardens which had been the private delight of so many Royal generations.

Today Windsor plays an important part in the lives of our Royal Family. It was from Windsor Castle that the ex-King Edward VIII made his historic broadcast in which he informed the Nation that he had abdicated. His father had been the first Sovereign of the House of Windsor and he himself took the name as the title for his Dukedom. The present Queen has perpetuated the dynasty. By proclamation on the 9th April 1952 she declared, 'her will and pleasure that she and her children shall be styled and known as the House and Family of Windsor'. It was a fitting gesture to history.

The Castle remains inescapably a monument to what has gone before. Portraits by Holbein, van Dyke and Canaletto hang on the walls as well as the famous Leonardo drawings and there are few generations of Royal home makers who have not left their mark in one way or another. In 1960 the Queen made her own contribution by having the interior of the Edward III tower remodelled. In one suite she decided to introduce a modern note which would be a memorial to her own times. Sir Hugh and Lady Casson were commissioned to design it entirely in the modern idiom. The furniture was submitted to the Furniture Makers' Guild and they set on it their seal of approval by granting awards to eighteen pieces. The Queen also selected twenty contemporary pictures for the suite – the largest ever Royal purchase

A room in the State Apartments: the desk was
used by Prince Albert

BATHROOM LINEN ROOM HOUSEKEEPERS ROOM

Queen Mary's famous
doll's-house at Windsor.
The paintings are real,
even the clocks work

State bedroom at Windsor

of modern art. Windsor is the sort of place where the old lives comfortably with the new.

Today the upper, middle and lower wards of the Castle spread over thirteen acres. Many Court officials still live within its walls. The Church is represented by a Dean and six canons and, as a reminder of its history as a fortress, there is a resident Governor and a military guard at the gates. It also provides a home for the Military Knights whose time-honoured role it is to deputise for the Garter Knights in St George's Chapel if they themselves cannot attend.

During the last two years Windsor has played an increasingly important part in the Royal routine. By tradition the Court assembles there for three to four weeks at Easter and again for two to three weeks in June but recently the Royal Family have selected it as the place to spend the Royal Christmas in preference to Sandringham. The reason for this is that it has become a much more satisfactory home for a growing family. Although much of the Castle is open to the public, the Royal Apartments have complete privacy and they can enjoy their favourite pastime of horse riding in the private parkland. Prince Philip and Prince Charles in particular look forward to their visits there to play polo in Windsor Great Park so that, apart from the Christmas visit, the Castle is being used more and more as a country retreat to be used at weekends and at a convenient distance from London.

Frogmore, one of the favourite and most elegant
retreats of the Queen

Windsor Gardens

When considering the Royal Gardens, Windsor must be accorded a special place, not for the pleasure gardens, fine though they are, but for the vast area devoted to supplying the Royal houses with flowers and vegetables.

There are few families in the country who do not acknowledge the value of having a vegetable patch of their own. The home-grown vegetables are generally considered as incomparably superior to those bought in a shop and this cannot entirely be put down to a natural pride in supplying the family table by one's own efforts. Young vegetables freshly picked each morning for the needs of the day *do* taste better. The Royal Family think so too but the problem of supplying their needs is indeed a complex one. Just consider what is required.

The Queen and Prince Philip spend by far the greater part of the year at one or other of their official residences – Windsor and Buckingham Palace. At both, but particularly the latter, they have a vast housekeeping problem because of the number of official guests whom they are required to entertain every year. It is a never-ending process, varying only in the numbers to be entertained every day – sometimes a small luncheon party, sometimes a great banquet. Add to this the large number of staff who have to be fed every day and it will be realised that the strain put on the 'family allotment' is a considerable one.

The vegetable gardens, the greenhouses and the flower gardens at Windsor which supply the Royal needs are, in fact, enormous. There are about twenty-four acres devoted to vegetables alone and another eight acres down to fruit. There are two acres of flowers to be cut for room decoration and only a slightly smaller area under glass. By any standards this is 'big business'.

Let us look first at the greenhouses. They are placed in rows, end to end, and connected by glass-enclosed corridors so that exotic plants can be moved from one to the other without exposing them to the rigours of the English climate. The houses themselves have another peculiar feature. Each end door is a large mirror so that the impression the visitor gets is of an endless vista stretching to infinity.

One of the main functions of the greenhouses is to provide all the year round floral decoration for Buckingham Palace and Windsor – no small task. There are climbing plants which grow in pots, like the tropical caladiums with their pretty foliage, the pink-blooming grape myrtle or the fantastic looking anthurium. A great favourite with the Queen are the orchids to which several houses are devoted. There is one house entirely devoted to the Cymbidiums and another to the Miltonias and so on. The Calanthe, a member of the orchid family, is particularly popular as it flowers profusely during the barren months of December and January. Another winter flower

which often decorates the Royal table at Christmas is the Mexican Poinsettia.

There is also a great deal of fruit produced under glass. The late fructifying Peregrine peach is a great favourite. There are several varieties of grapes and even plums which are not normally regarded as a hothouse fruit. Most of the fruit is, however, grown out of doors. All the well-known apples are represented in the orchards like Cox's Orange Pippin and Bramley Seedling, as well as several lesser known ones like Tower of Glamis which gets its name from the Queen Mother's family home in Scotland. There is an equally fine selection of pear trees from the well known Conference to the more unusual Trout which is speckled like a fish.

Guests at Buckingham Palace often remark afterwards, not on the richness of the meal, for the Royal Family prefer plain food beautifully cooked, but on the wonderful flavour of the vegetables. It is a great compliment to the gardeners at Windsor – and to the fact that the Queen always insists on her vegetables being pulled while they are young and tender. They are sent in by van every morning and cooked the same day. All the usual vegetables are grown but the Royal preference is extended to some which many people affect to despise. The humble turnip for example finds a regular place on their menu. They are pulled when they are scarcely the size of a cricket ball and are delicious. Indeed to see the daily consignment of vegetables is to imagine that they might have been grown in a doll's garden. The onions are button sized, the carrots only a couple of inches long and even cauliflowers, which so many gardeners take pride in growing to giant size, are gathered whilst they are still tiny.

Many varieties of soft fruit are also grown – strawberries, raspberries, currants and gooseberries in particular. Others, like crab apples and quinces, go straight to the housekeeper's department to be made into jams and jellies, for the principles of good housekeeping are rigorously observed in the Royal homes. Add to this the great quantity of cut flowers which are sent up every day to decorate the public rooms of the Palace as well as the private Royal Apartments and it will be seen what a very considerable responsibility rests on the head gardener at Windsor. He lives, incidentally, in a charming house in the centre of his domain where there is a room set aside for the Queen should she wish to rest or have a cup of tea during one of her periodical tours of inspection.

The gardens at Windsor are, however, not entirely devoted to the practical needs of the Royal Family.

The flower beds and Orangery known as the East Terrace have already been mentioned in passing. In addition to the ever changing floral scene, there are some delightful as well as unusual shrubs and trees. There is, for example, a Pomegranate as well as a free flowering Magnolia with unusually dark coloured blooms. There is also Orange Blossom and Lemon Scented Verbena as well as many others which make the East Terrace Gardens particularly

Left:
The Queen's favourite pastime: riding in Windsor Great Park

Previous page:
Herbaceous border at Windsor

delightful – and also a convenient retreat for the Royal Family, for the Orangery now contains a modern swimming-bath and Prince Philip has installed a wooden horse on which he sits to practise his polo shots.

There is another garden within the area covered by Windsor Castle which is worth mention although, strictly speaking, it is not a Royal garden as it is for the use of the Lieutenant Governor of the Castle who lives in the Norman Tower. It lies to the south-west of the Tower and has a delightful air of informality. It rises and falls with the contours of the ground with niches off the wandering path where benches and arbours are placed from which one can enjoy the view. As pretty a garden as one could wish to see, bright with flowers and made gayer by the little stream which tumbles from pool to pool.

Outside the Castle walls, over on the east side of the Great Park, lie the Savill Gardens. They used to be called the Woodland Gardens until George VI ordered that the name be changed to honour Major Eric Savill who had worked with the King for many years to build up a wonderful collection of plants there. These gardens are built around two interconnected ponds, planted about with a great variety of irises and water lilies. It is ideal soil for rhododendrons and azaleas which were amongst George VI's favourites. The gardens are, in fact, a carefully planned display of attractive trees and shrubs which are complemented by herbaceous plants massed in great double beds. In the north-west corner of the gardens are the propagating nurseries which exist to keep up the supply of thousands of plants and shrubs and spring bulbs which make a wonderful display in their season.

Azaleas at Windsor

George VI was a great gardener and has left his mark on most of the Royal gardens. None, however, more so than the gardens of Royal Lodge which is hidden away in the south-east corner of Windsor Great Park. As a Royal grace and favour residence, it was his home for many years and it is here in the gardens that *Y Bwthyn Bach*, the little house presented to the Princesses by the people of Wales, stands.

George VI's great achievement at Royal Lodge must be counted as the opening up of the gardens so that there is an atmosphere of spaciousness, splendid vistas and room for the very fine trees and shrubs to be admired. He was, above all, interested in landscaping and understood the subject exceptionally well. He abominated fussiness with so much 'going on' that you literally could not see the wood for the trees.

Royal Lodge has a splendid lawn stretching away from the terrace in front of the house and, at the end of the lawn, four beautifully proportioned maple trees. The great expanse of lawn is broken up by a huge clump of yellow rhododendrons. The view from the saloon at the right of the house is dominated by two majestic Lebanon cedars and on the left a remarkable oak tree with a girth of twenty-one feet. There are many other fine trees scattered throughout the grounds and acting as a backcloth to magnificent avenues of rhododendrons and azaleas. The oaks are remarkably fine but the

Narcissus in the woodland at Windsor

Above:
Herbaceous border at
Windsor

Left:
Frogmore: an Indian temple
from Lucknow, presented to
Queen Victoria

most unusual is probably the huge eucalyptus. It is only about thirty years old but has already reached a height of over fifty feet. There are glades of miniature daffodils and other spring flowers and even a glade made up entirely of camellias.

Before ending this short survey of the Royal Gardens at Windsor, there is just one human note which might be added – the sort of small detail which means so much in a well loved family garden. It springs from a tradition observed in the Royal Family that their wedding bouquets should always contain a few sprigs of myrtle. After the wedding they are given to the Head Gardener at Royal Lodge to plant so that the tubs of myrtle which are to be seen there have a very special significance.

Sandringham

Each of the Royal residences has an individuality of its own, but perhaps none more so than Sandringham House. Buckingham Palace can never entirely escape from the officialdom which surrounds it. Windsor is redolent with the history of a thousand years and Balmoral bears the ineradicable stamp of Queen Victoria and Prince Albert who created it and made it for ever their own.

There is nothing official about Sandringham; it has little or no history and Queen Victoria only visited it twice in her lifetime. Yet it is a much loved Royal House. 'Dear old Sandringham' wrote George V, 'the place I love better than anywhere else in the world.' It is a sentiment which Edward VII would certainly have seconded. So would George VI.

The acquisition of Sandringham by the Royal Family is due to one of them who never lived there. Prince Albert had, for many years, foreseen that his eldest son would require a house of his own. He had set aside for the purpose a large part of the income from the Duchy of Cornwall which he controlled during the minority of the Prince of Wales. When the chance of acquiring Sandringham occurred in 1861, the usually careful Prince Consort plunged in with an offer of £220,000.

It was altogether a surprising decision and not the least because the negotiations for the sale were conducted by Lord Palmerston on behalf of the owner who was his stepson the Hon. Charles Spencer Cowper. There was little love lost between the Prince and Palmerston whom the Prince once described as '. . . an indefatigable man of business . . . no very high standard of honour and not a grain of moral feeling'. Palmerston certainly drove a hard bargain. The price paid was exceptionally high by the standards of the day, the situation of the house remote and its condition such that it was necessary to set aside a further sum of £60,000 to bring it up to date. Before the famous agriculturalist Coke of Norfolk (later the Earl of Leicester) had introduced new farming methods on the neighbouring estate of Holkham, it had been said of the thin, sandy Norfolk soil that there were two rabbits competing for every single blade of grass which grew there.

The house itself was a long, low unpretentious building faced with shabby stucco and adorned with mock Elizabethan chimneys. A third attic storey imposed on the ground and first floor, threw the whole edifice out of proportion, giving it an ungainly appearance. It looked out over the bleak Wolferton marshes and the often desolate prospect of the Wash and little attempt had been made to beautify the 200-acre park.

A few months after he had concluded the purchase the Prince Consort died, but not before his eldest son was able to tell him of his enthusiasm for

Sandringham House, the most intimate of all the Royal Family's homes his new home. The young Prince of Wales had taken an immediate liking to the place and at once started to make plans for its improvement.

When he married two years later, the house took on an even greater importance in the lives of the young couple. There had been much gossip about the wild parties which the Prince liked to give at Marlborough House and of the pace he set in London Society. At Sandringham, however, he was a different person. W. T. Stead, in the *Review of Reviews*, expressed the feeling of a slightly shocked nation when he wrote, 'It would be as the breath of Heaven, if the air of Sandringham could be brought to Marlborough House'.

It was not to say, however, that life at Sandringham was dull. The Prince of Wales and his Princess loved to entertain there and the house was always full to overflowing with guests. They were a cosmopolitan lot. The local Norfolk squires were invited to meet European Society. Bankers and business-men, artists and musicians were all invited to make the train journey to King's Lynn and drive in carriages over the rutted roads to spend long weekends with 'the first gentleman in the land'.

Soon, as was so frequently discovered in homes acquired by the Royal Family, it was decided that the house was altogether too small for its purpose. Practically the whole ungainly building was pulled down and building started afresh. The house we see today was the result – a solid red brick building with three times the number of bedrooms it had had before but somehow achieving a much more elegant line. The architect was Albert Jenkins Humbert, a man of no very great ability but one who had, in Prince Albert's eyes, the inestimable advantage that he would do what he was told! Under the Prince's eager directions he incorporated a billiards room and a ballroom, a library and some fine reception rooms. When he discovered that the Earl of Leicester had a game room at Holkham where 1,300 birds could be hung at the same time, the Prince insisted that Sandringham should have a bigger one. To cap it all he had an American-style bowling alley constructed and made sound-proof so that the men could enjoy their game after the ladies had retired to bed.

Outside the house, great improvements to the grounds were put in hand. Trees were cut down to make room for a splendid sweep of lawn and a broad drive created leading to the Norwich Gates on the north side of the park. A shallow lake suitable for skating in the winter was provided and, on the Wolferton marshes, the Prince had another pond constructed where he could indulge one of his favourite sports of flighting duck. The park was filled with fallow deer and even with some red deer from Balmoral which, surprisingly, survived their transportation from their native hills.

Finally he turned his attention to his 7,000-acre estate which, in the time of the impecunious Cowper, had been allowed to fall into a disgraceful state of disrepair. Unlike Holkham, which was one of the most advanced agricultural estates in the country, the Sandringham tenants lived in antiquated

Sandringham

A rare picture of Queen Victoria's own drawing-room at Sandringham. Note the crown in the foreground

The King's study at Sandringham, as it was fifty
years ago. Few photographs of the house during
this period exist

houses which were sometimes little better than hovels and no money had been spent on the farm buildings for many years. The Prince undertook his obligations as a Norfolk squire with enthusiasm, and if there were complaints that he paid more attention to improving the sporting amenities of the estate than its agricultural potential it was no more than other Norfolk squires were prone to do.

There were other, more exotic, 'improvements' to the estate. An enormous, Chinese Buddha was smuggled back from China aboard the *Rodney* by Admiral Keppel and presented to the Prince. It was installed in one of the glades in the gardens where it has continued to smile blandly to the present day. Both the Prince and the Princess had sunken baths each carved from a single, vast block of marble – white marble for the Princess, black for the Prince, and representing the height of sybaritic comfort. They even, on a trip to Egypt, took a fancy to 'an intelligent, ugly little boy, not very black, with a large silver ring stuck in one ear'. They brought him back to Sandringham with them where he became almost as much of a despot as John Brown had been to Queen Victoria's households. He eventually overstepped the mark by borrowing one of the Prince's sporting guns which he managed to break before returning it surreptitiously to its case. It was too much for the Prince who found him another job with one of his friends – a rather Greek gift.

In spite of the happiness the Royal couple found at Sandringham, there was also sadness. Only four months after the great party given for the house warming of the new house, Princess Alexandra's sixth child was born there. He lived for only twenty-four hours. Eight months later, Albert Edward himself contracted typhoid during a shooting party in Yorkshire. He returned to Sandringham where he nearly died. Queen Victoria hurried to his bedside, which was the first time she had visited the house. The Duke of Cambridge was sure that the fever had been caught at Sandringham and that the drains were bad. He detected, he claimed, a bad smell in the library but it was subsequently discovered to be due to a gas leak.

Although Princess Alexandra never made it an excuse for not going there, the house affected her rheumatism badly and sometimes she was so crippled that she could not mount her horse.

In spite of these misfortunes, however, it was a house where there was great fun to be had. The recurring theme in the memories of people who visited Sandringham is of the relaxed and gay atmosphere. There were impromptu dances to a barrel organ which the Prince loved to operate himself. On more formal occasions he would lead the revels, never missing a dance and keeping it up until the small hours of the morning by which time most of the guests would be utterly exhausted.

Most of all Sandringham has earned its place in the Royal affections for the fine sport which the estate provides. It used to be one of the finest partridge shoots in England and still holds a high place as a pheasant shoot.

York Cottage, Sandringham

Much of its pre-eminence was due to Albert Edward who knew every copse and spinney and he raised it from an average shoot to one where as many as twenty-eight thousand head were shot in a season.

For succeeding generations the pattern of life set at Sandringham will always be associated with Albert Edward and Princess Alexandra whose portrait still dominates the main drawing room. It was bought as a private house and a private house it has remained both in spirit and practice – a place for happy weekends, for shooting parties and all the other entertainments usual in an English country home. When Edward VII died as a result of catching cold one wet afternoon when he insisted on going out to see what progress had been made with his tree planting plans on the estate, he was succeeded by George V, who was already deeply imbued with a love of the place. By then Sandringham had belonged to the Royal Family for almost fifty years and for seventeen of those his home had been at York Cottage in the Sandringham grounds.

There can never have been a more 'unlikely' Royal home than York Cottage. It was originally built as an annexe to the big house and was known as Bachelor's Cottage until, in 1893, Albert Edward made it over to his eldest son. In appearance it is indistinguishable from a stockbroker's suburban villa with its stained glass fanlights and mock tudor beams. Surrounded by gloomy laurel bushes, it stands down by the lake a few hundred yards from Sandringham itself. It was the honeymoon home to which George brought his bride Princess Mary and it must have been quite a shock to her, with her love of the traditional, to discover that he had furnished it from top to toe with shiny new furniture from one of London's more modern emporiums. Only in his own study had he departed from the conventional by having the walls of that already dark room 'papered' with scarlet cloth 'of the type used for the trousers of the French army'. It was a miracle how the whole household and their retainers fitted into such a small house. When asked how it was managed, the Duke of York is supposed to have replied that he imagined the servants slept in trees!

The stables at Sandringham House with Derby-winner Persimmon

Yet the Yorks loved their cottage and kept it on for many years after their accession. It was there that all their children were born with the exception of the Duke of Windsor and it was there that they were largely brought up to enjoy the country pursuits which had become a Sandringham tradition. George V was above all things a traditionalist and he even carried it into the bringing up of his family. 'My father was frightened of his mother,' he once said, 'I was frightened of my father, and I am d——d well going to see that my children are frightened of me.' He even kept on the tradition started by Edward VII of 'Sandringham time'. Edward, with his love of punctuality, had decreed that the clocks should be kept an hour fast at Sandringham and George continued the practice.

There was one innovation at Sandringham which was owed to George V – the Christmas broadcast when he spoke to his subjects more as the head of a

big family than as a Monarch. There could be no more suitable setting for this annual message of goodwill than Sandringham. The Duke of Windsor once described Christmases at Sandringham as 'Dickens in a Cartier setting' but it was the warm atmosphere of a Dickensian family Christmas which the King managed to convey in his broadcasts, rather than formality.

Sandringham was very much 'home' to King George yet, oddly enough, he only used the house for the last ten years of his reign. He remained content with his York Cottage and left it to his mother to remain as mistress of the house which she had helped to create. She died there in 1925, spending her last day discussing with her comptroller what improvements should be made.

In 1935, scarcely a month after his Christmas day broadcast and the celebrating of his Silver Jubilee, the final bulletin was issued from Sandringham that 'The King's life is moving peacefully to its close'. He died as he

would have liked to live – a country squire surrounded by all the things he loved best.

Edward VIII did not share the family enthusiasm for the country life. He was quite content to remain at Fort Belvedere and preferred fox hunting to shooting. With his passion for modernity, his first act was to order the abolition of 'Sandringham time'. It was symptomatic of the new regime. For a long time he had regarded Sandringham as an archaic survival of a bygone age and an unnecessary drain on the private royal purse. He resented the considerable sum of money which was devoted to rearing game birds and impatient when he found that an experimental flax farm which his father had started was losing money. He at once ordered economies to take

Previous page:
Some of the Queen's prize-winning cattle at Sandringham

place and appointed experts to discover ways and means of achieving them. Many of them were carried out after his abdication.

George VI by contrast bore all the love for Sandringham of his father and grandfather. When he assumed the tenancy (for the house was still owned by Queen Mary) he brought with him a breath of fresh air to the Edwardian atmosphere. It became once again a house for young people. Lady Airlie, Queen Mary's old lady-in-waiting, records this in her memoirs in describing a visit under the new regime. 'In the entrance hall there now stood a baize-covered table on which jigsaw puzzles were laid out. The younger members of the party, the Princesses . . . and several young Guardsmen congregated round them from morning to night. The radio, worked by Princess Elizabeth, blared incessantly.' Although his bowling alley had long since disappeared, one feels that Edward VII would definitely have approved.

It was to Sandringham that Prince Philip came as a young naval officer to spend his first Christmas leave and it was there that he first learned the delights of pheasant shooting – now one of his favourite sports. It was to Sandringham that Prince Charles was sent to spend Christmas when, in 1950, Princess Elizabeth went to join Philip in Malta. 'He is too sweet stumping around the room', the King wrote to his daughter. 'We shall love having him at Sandringham. He is the fifth generation to live there and I hope he will get to love the place.' Later he wrote to Queen Mary, 'I want Lilibet and Philip to get to know it too as I have always been so happy here.'

The following year he, like his father, died there. He had been out shooting hares the day before and killed three with his last three shots.

Today Sandringham is the sole property of the Queen. The estate of 7,000 acres has now grown to almost 20,000 and comprises some of the most valuable land in the country. The Royal shooting parties are still held there but, much as Prince Philip loves the sport, the rearing of game takes second place to the needs of agriculture. When the Queen or Prince Philip visit agricultural shows, they look at the exhibits with the eyes of experts. All manner of experiments have been tried from patent carrot-washing machines to mushroom growing and Prince Philip himself has been known to act as a salesman for the frozen peas produced on the estate.

Perhaps, for the Queen, the greatest outside interest at Sandringham is the Royal Stud which was founded by Edward VII and today provides her with both an enduring interest and a source of considerable profit.

Two years ago there came a break with tradition. The Queen decided that with a growing family and the pressing needs of State, the Royal Christmas could be more conveniently managed at Windsor than at Sandringham. Many people will regret the change but it is typical of the Royal Family that practical considerations should supersede sentiment. That their attachment to the house, which celebrates its centenary as a Royal residence in 1968, remains unimpaired is beyond all doubt.

The Queen is one of the foremost owners of thorough-bred cattle in Britain. These rosettes, at Sandringham, are just a few of the recent awards

Sandringham Gardens

All the Royal gardens have their own characteristics and Sandringham is no exception. As the Queen's private country estate it is just like many others of greater or lesser splendour up and down the country and there is no aspect which more clearly demonstrates this than the gardens. There is the house itself set in its park and, as in most country houses of the period, all the serious gardening is conducted behind high brick walls. Certainly the scale on which the Sandringham walled gardens are laid out is more impressive than most but the pattern is strictly traditional. It does not make them any less interesting, particularly in these days when fewer and fewer of the big families feel able to keep up their gardens in the grand style laid down by their forefathers who did not have to worry too much about the number of gardeners they employed in the process.

The gardens at Sandringham are divided into two main parts, the East Garden and the West, with a road running in between. Let us look first at the East Garden which includes the glass houses, the kitchen garden out of which opens the Dairy Garden and, its most striking feature, the herbaceous border.

The herbaceous border is really astonishing in its size. The main path is three hundred and ten yards long and twelve feet wide. The borders extend to another twelve feet on either side and, in the true English tradition, are backed by fruit trees, designed to conceal the vegetable gardens which lie behind. The number of plants required to fill these vast beds is as impressive as their variety. Antirrhinums and fuchsias, petunias, godetias and scabious to name only a few annuals are planted out each year to mingle with the perennials which grow in great clumps of bewildering variety. Like all well planned herbaceous borders, they are planted so that the shorter-stemmed flowers show in front with the taller ones ranged behind to form a bank of colour where the varieties are so cleverly mixed that the eye never tires of one shade or shape. Acres of vegetable beds lie concealed beyond and round the walls are trained fruit trees of every variety. In spite of the blaze of colour which greets the visitor to this walled garden it is known as the main vegetable garden. Beyond it there is a smaller walled garden which is known as 'The Chalks' and which is also mainly devoted to vegetables although, at first sight, the rambler roses which are trained over iron railings almost conceal its real purpose.

Beyond The Chalks, there is a delightful little garden known as the Dairy Garden and, indeed, it is adjoined by the Royal Dairies. This garden used to be a favourite retreat of Queen Alexandra. She used to walk there from the house to take tea amongst the trees pruned into the shape of birds of all sizes and descriptions and enjoy the scent of the lilacs and double-flowered almond trees.

The lake in the grounds of Sandringham

The giant pergola in the Sandringham walled
garden

The ornamental garden at
Sandringham

There are other features of the East Gardens which are worthy of note. There is the great pergola in what is known as the Square Garden and which leads on to the herbaceous border. The pergola is of massive construction. There are brick piers placed every fifteen feet to support the cross timbers which are of formidable size. Half way along – its length is seventy yards – the bays widen out to form an octagon in the centre of which stands an attractive Italian well head. The marble seats round the sides are the work of Sir Lawrence Alma Tadema. The great pergola itself forms a climbing frame for clematis and wisteria, honeysuckle, roses and purple-leaved vine.

The greenhouses are divided into two main sections, one of which concentrates on plants and the other on fruits.

The plant houses are known as the Persimmon range and for a good reason. Edward VI's famous horse Persimmon won the Derby and the King used the money to build the greenhouses. The amount he won must have been substantial for no expense has been spared. The woodwork throughout is solid teak and should last virtually for ever. In the winter the plant houses are filled with chrysanthemums to be used over Christmas in the Royal homes or sent to the surrounding hospitals. By the beginning of summer, when

Previous page:
Sandringham

88

visitors are admitted to the gardens and greenhouses, they are a blaze of colour. Early on the cinerarias and scented stocks are particularly fine. Later on the hydrangeas, fuchsias and geraniums come into their own.

In the fruit houses all manner of fruits are grown but a special mention must be given to the peach trees. They are particularly fine both in the fruit they give and in the way they are trained along the back walls of the glass houses.

To cross the road into the West Gardens is to enter a different world. Here is the country house park at its best. It was not always so majestic as it appears today for, in Edward VII's time, the great expanse was broken up by the planting of clumps of trees. The idea was that, from whatever direction the wind blew, there was always some shelter to be found. George VI, with his love of landscaping, swept these not very attractive clumps away and had the whole park grassed over, allowing only a few fine specimen trees to remain. The result has been that the views from the house have been greatly enhanced.

In former days, the drive from the great Norwich Gate, by which the public now enter, used to lead straight to the house along a magnificent avenue of lime trees. Unfortunately they were almost all blown down in a great storm in 1908. The reconstructed drive was diverted to achieve greater privacy and later George VI constructed the great bank of cotoneasters, cypresses, berberis and forsythia which is such an attractive feature today as well as achieving even greater privacy.

An important feature of the West Gardens is the lake. Although it was largely artificially created, it now fits naturally into the scene. Azaleas, magnolias and berberis grow around its shores and, at one place, even bamboo thrives in the sandy soil. It makes a wonderful haven for the waterfowl which Edward VII loved so much.

To the west of the house lies the Church Walk, a long pine-bordered avenue which leads to the Church and the Old Deer Park. Apart from the avenue itself, most of the trees planted in this part of the park have a special significance. Many have been planted by visiting Royalty, dating back as far as 1872. One group of oaks was raised from acorns picked up on the battlefield at Verdun in 1917 and so on.

Most impressive of all is the atmosphere of the Sandringham gardens. They have the leisured air of a bygone age and yet there is a purposefulness about them. Where rows of gardeners once tilled the vegetable beds by hand, rotavators now hold sway. Of recent years there has been a streamlining in all departments to bring them into line with the efficient agricultural estate of which they are the hub. Prince Philip takes great interest in the opportunities offered by intensive market gardening with the result that there is always some new equipment being tried out to prepare the produce more efficiently for market. That is Sandringham – a forward-looking place, steeped in tradition but with one foot firmly placed in the twentieth century.

A rare photograph of the Royal pets' corner at Sandringham

Balmoral

At the end of August 1842, Queen Victoria and Prince Albert paid their first visit to Scotland. It was a journey which was to have far reaching effects, not only on their own lives, but on the whole of Scotland.

On this memorable visit they stayed at Taymouth Castle with the Marquis of Bredalbane, one of Scotland's biggest landowners. It was said of him that he could walk a hundred miles in a straight line without ever setting foot off his own land. At Taymouth they fell in love with Scotland and it was probably on that first visit that they decided to find a house of their own amongst the rugged hills. It was, for them, to be more than a house. It was to be their retreat from the stiff formality of their daily lives – a place where they could relax and lead a family life without having to conform to the exacting demands of Court etiquette.

Other visits to Scotland followed but it was not until five years later, in 1847, that the Royal couple discovered the spot which was to be their future home in the highlands – and become the number one attraction for future generations of Scottish tourists.

At first Balmoral was taken on lease from the Earl of Mar. It stood on the site of an older house and had only been completed as a residence for Sir Robert Gordon in 1839. As Scottish baronial houses go it was small. On the ground floor, apart from the domestic quarters, there was only a hall, a billiards room and a dining room with a fine broad staircase leading up to a drawing room on the first floor and the Royal bedrooms. The ladies and gentlemen in their retinue had to make do with the small, box-like rooms on the two floors above. With the Queen, however, it was a case of love at first sight. She was fascinated by the wild grandeur of Lochnagar which towered above the castle and by the silvery waters of the River Dee which flowed near its walls. Above all she was in love with the solitude. The railhead was still thirty-five miles away at Banchory and the journey from London was a long and onerous one.

The Royal Family continued to live in their cramped quarters for four years, returning faithfully each summer for a long holiday. In 1852 they managed to buy the house and estate. With 17,400 acres reaching to the summit of Lochnagar the price was £31,500. It was a purchase which has never been regretted by succeeding generations of the Royal Family.

As soon as the castle came into Royal ownership, work was put in hand to transform it into something more suitable than the mere 'laird's house' which it had been. 'Transform' is perhaps not the right word for the first step was to demolish the old house and start afresh. It is often supposed that Prince Albert was the architect of the new house – a view which is supported

Balmoral, summer home of the Royal Family

by the Queen herself who wrote in *Leaves from the Journal of Our Life in the Highlands*, '. . . my dearest Albert's own creation, own work, own building, own laying-out, as at Osborne'. In fact, the architect was William Smith of Aberdeen whose father, John Smith, had built Sir William Gordon's house. It was built from the local, attractively light-coloured granite, hewn from a nearby quarry which has, alas, recently become worked out.

It is fashionable today to laugh at the Neo-Baronial style in which Balmoral was built and which was the vogue in the nineteenth century; nonetheless it remains a fine example of the builder's art. Of William Smith's handling of the native stone, Dr Douglas Simpson wrote; 'He never tormented it with effects for which the material is unsuited, but boldly massed his rock-like masonry so that his buildings have something of the hard crystalline character proper to the stone. Above all, he was rigorous in his insistence on good craftmanship. Everything about his buildings – masonry, woodwork, plaster, cast-iron and lead – is of the highest quality and the most enduring character.' It is a good description of Balmoral. Certainly he adorned it with a fortress-like square tower, set on top with pinnacles, towers and turrets, but inside he created a house which was very much a home. The dining room and drawing rooms are of modest size and the whole effect not nearly so pretentious as is to be found in many of the other large houses which people were having built at about the same time. He built his house round a quadrangle and, bearing in mind that the Queen would from time to time have to hold large-scale entertainments there, created one large ballroom which is sixty-eight feet by twenty-five. It is the room which the present Queen now uses most often as a private cinema.

Queen Victoria and Prince Albert were not so restrained when it came to decorating the interior. They had both an immense admiration for all things Scottish and the décor certainly reflected their taste. Tartan was used wherever possible. There were tartan furnishings and tartan curtains and there was even tartan linoleum. The tartans most frequently used were the extremely bright Royal Stuart and the less garish Hunting Stuart but Prince Albert was not content with these alone. He designed a Balmoral tartan of black, red and lavender. The present Duke of Edinburgh had a kilt made of this material in which he appeared for the first time at the Balmoral Games in 1952.

Where tartan was not used on the walls, the Queen had flocked wallpaper designed on which the Royal Cipher was embossed. To add to the Scottish effect, mounted stags' heads were hung in great profusion around the walls and the fashionable painter Landseer was commissioned to paint huge canvasses depicting Scottish scenes and the Royal family portraits against a Scottish background. The Queen was accustomed to drive out in a tartan-decked barouche and even the carry-lamps used to light guests to their bedrooms were designed in the shape of figures of Highlanders.

The Royal taste in decoration set off a fashion which swept Scotland.

Aerial view of the castle showing the private lawns and gardens in the foreground

A delightful engraving of the Queen's sitting room
at Balmoral

An engraving of Prince Albert's sitting room at
Balmoral

Everyone who could lay claim to a tartan, and many who could not, blossomed out in kilts. Highland sports became a 'must' for people with social aspirations and to attend Highland Games became the smart thing to do. Much fun has since been poked at what Sir Compton Mackenzie was later to dub 'Balmorality' but there is no doubt that the establishment of a Royal home in the Highlands has had a lasting effect on the prosperity of the whole of Scotland.

The foundation stone of the new Balmoral was laid with great ceremony on 28th September 1853. It contained a cavity in which a parchment was placed signed by all the Royal Family. The life of the new house had begun and by the time it was ready for occupation in 1855 it at once started to play its part in history. It was to Balmoral that the news was brought to the Queen of the fall of Sebastopol and a great bonfire was lit on the top of Craig Gowan. The Queen and her Consort joined whole-heartedly in the celebrations which followed, at which the bagpipes were played, much whisky was drunk and the wild Highlanders let their guns off far into the night.

In the same year Prince Fredrick of Prussia travelled to Balmoral and proposed to the Queen's eldest daughter (Princess Victoria) on a walk up the nearby Glen Girnoch. The eldest son of their marriage became Kaiser Wilhelm II who went to war against England in 1914.

Queen Victoria and Prince Albert set a pattern of living at Balmoral which has been followed by their successors and in which the outdoor life played an important part. The Queen made extraordinarily arduous journeys in the surrounding hills and Prince Albert spent long days hunting the stags with which the countryside abounds. Remote though it was, however, their privacy could never quite be complete. There was entertaining to be done and affairs of State to be attended to even on holidays. Gladstone paid many visits there and Disraeli made the long journey twice, each time going down with a heavy cold.

Queen Victoria had not been long established at Balmoral before she was casting covetous eyes at some of the surrounding property. The first place to claim her attention was ancient Abergeldie Castle which stands at the side of the Dee about two miles from Crathie. It belonged to the Gordon family and is one of Scotland's finest castles as well as one of the oldest. It dates from around 1200. Unfortunately, the Gordons were not of a mind to sell it but eventually the Queen managed to obtain a long lease on it and it became second in importance only to Balmoral as a Royal house. Queen Victoria's mother lived there from 1850–7 and it has had many Royal residents since. Down the years a great deal of Royal money was spent on improving the castle and in beautifying the grounds so that today it is one of the show places of the north. It is open to the public on certain days and is well worth visiting as much for the beauty of the gardens as the dramatic interior of the castle itself.

Gamekeeper's cottage – known as 'Teapot Cottage' at Glensheil, Balmoral. It was given to Princess Margaret by her mother and is used for picnics during grouse shooting

With the death of the Prince, the carefree atmosphere of Balmoral changed. For the Queen it became more a shrine to her beloved Albert than anything else. Where before it had provided her with an escape from routine, she now imposed a routine on her courtiers which was more than ever strict. She spent as long as five months in every year there and they were apt to be months of gloom for the Household officials who were not allowed to be visited even by their wives. Smoking was only permitted from the hour of leaving the dining room at 11 pm until the smoking room was closed by the Queen's orders on the stroke of midnight.

Edward VII, although he liked the opportunities for sport which Balmoral provided, really had his heart in Sandringham. His visits to the north were regular but did not last nearly as long as his mother's. The attitude of George V and Queen Mary was much the same. Perhaps all the children and grand-children had suffered too much from the gloomy routine which clouded the old Queen's last years in the house she had created in the first flush of love. Edward VII had so disliked his mother's trusted companion John Brown that when he succeeded he ordered the cairns which had been erected in his memory to be pulled down. Queen Mary as Princess May of Teck had written to her husband in 1895. 'I like Balmoral for about a fortnight, but I honestly think that longer than that is rather an ordeal for the everlasting questions and the carefulness of one's replies is extremely fatiguing in the long run.'

The castle took on a new lease of life when George VI and Queen Elizabeth succeeded to the throne. The new King liked the role of a Highland laird and he showed as great and as intimate an interest in his tenants as his great grandmother. 'I know so much about the place', he once wrote, 'I feel I am part of it. I like the people and I believe they like me.' Towards the end of his reign, as his health began to fail, he sought refuge more and more at Balmoral. Its health-giving atmosphere did as much to prolong his life as the visits to Bognor had achieved for George V.

Crathie Church, Balmoral, from the Royal Estate

When the present Queen inherited the castle she too inherited a deep love for it and for the surrounding countryside. With the speed of modern communications it is not nearly so cut off as it used to be but it is still suf-ficiently remote to provide a restful holiday. Soon after her accession there were rumours that the days of Balmoral as a Royal Home were numbered. They were at once denied. Since then both she and the Duke have demon-strated, in many ways, the high regard she has for her Highland estates.

When the Duke first married, it is doubtful whether he had ever held a shotgun in his hands. Certainly he was not proficient in the art of shooting which had become something of a Royal tradition. Edward VII was num-bered as one of the finest shots in the country and George V was nearly as good. It was on the grouse moors of Balmoral that the Duke first mastered the difficult art and it is now one of the chief attractions of Balmoral for him.

In addition to the large acreage of moor which the Queen owns, they rent another big shoot from the Farquharsons of nearby Invercauld.

Another favourite sport for the Royal family is fishing for salmon in the Dee. It is a hobby from which both the Princesses and the Queen herself derive a great deal of pleasure and they are a familiar sight on the river bank. In fact, they find much of the pleasures of an open air life which Queen Victoria first discovered at Balmoral and delight in the informal atmosphere which allows them to drop in on their tenants for tea and roam the country-side at will. It is now their custom to visit Balmoral once a year, for a long holiday in August and September. Although they are generous in giving their time to opening factories and visiting various Scottish institutions when they are in the north, and in spite of the constant attention which has to be given to State affairs, Balmoral is a real holiday home. The names of guests invited to stay there are never published for the entertaining which is done is regarded in the light of private house parties and all formality is cut to a minimum.

When they first inherited the house – it is, of course, the private property of the Queen – they found it virtually unaltered from the days when it was first decorated by an enthusiastic Queen Victoria and Prince Albert. By and large they have left it much as they found it. There is still a profusion of tartan, now somewhat mellowed by time, and stags' heads still hang on the walls amidst the pictures by Landseer and Winterhalter. Some modernisation has, however, taken place but this has for the most part been concerned with improving the plumbing and dealing with the eternal problem in Royal Houses of trying to keep the place warm.

Now the time taken to fly from London to Aberdeen makes the long journey of olden days by train and coach seem to have been a trial indeed; but modern times have also brought with them modern problems. A million tourists flock to Royal Deeside every year and the road from the castle to Crathie Church is lined every Sunday morning with crowds of sightseers. Worse, the great hurricane which swept Scotland in 1953 and felled trees by the million also deprived the castle grounds of much of their privacy. The curious who cared to arm themselves with binoculars or cameras with telephoto lenses found no difficulty in intruding on the Royal Family's hard-won seclusion. Recently an elaborate arrangement of camouflage netting has done something to repair the situation until the newly planted trees can attain sufficient height.

Recently, too, a nine-hole golf course has been constructed in the grounds for the entertainment of guests who find the sport to be had in the hills to be too rigorous but that is one of the few concessions to modernity. All in all it has changed little from the 'my dear Balmoral' of Queen Victoria's day. One certainly feels that she would have approved of the enjoyment the present Royal Family derive from it.

The Queen is an expert fisherwoman, and the Balmoral stretch of the Dee is one of Scotland's finest salmon rivers

The wall garden of Balmoral, facing south

Balmoral Gardens

Balmoral is set amidst such dramatic scenery that there is a danger of the gardens providing an anti-climax. It is a place where one can stretch one's eyes to the summit of the hills like Craig Gowan or the even more imposing Lochnagar. In the summer the hills are aflame with colour and even in the winter the russets and browns have an ever-changing beauty of their own. Closer to the castle are the tall sentinel fir trees and the graceful silver birch. There is the majesty of the river Dee, sometimes in roaring spate and sometimes so low that it would seem an easy matter to wade across it. How can the ingenuity of man improve upon such a grand design?

The Royal gardeners at Balmoral have certainly been set a problem and they have aquitted themselves well. Everything from the three acre sweep of lawn to the massive splashes of colour provided by the flower beds have been generously conceived. There is nothing mean or fussy about the Balmoral Gardens.

One of the surprising things about the gardens is the way in which the flowers, fruit and vegetables flourish. In spite of its height above sea level and the northerly latitude many plants seem to do much better than further south. Strawberries, for example, grow to a great size and commonly yield more than a pound of fruit on each root. Raspberry canes attain a height of up to eight feet and are equally fruitful and there are many other examples of the plenteousness of nature high up in the fertile valley of the Dee.

The gardens themselves are quite small by Royal standards – not more than about ten acres – and they are planned to be at their best when the Royal Family come north for their long summer holiday. The general scheme aims at achieving its effect by the bold use of great clumps of flowers. If, for example, it is decided to plant out a bed with stocks, they are planted in great profusion so that no earth can be seen between the plants and the resulting splash of colour is magnificent.

Although the main preoccupation is to achieve a splendid overall effect which sets off the magnificent vistas, there is also a great attention to detail in the geometrical designs of the flower beds and the careful symmetry which can be seen to advantage in, for example, the pansy garden. There are also many items of individual interest to the flower lover. There is, for example, a particularly interesting rose which grows to the right of the porticoed front entrance to the Castle. This is generally known as the Bonnie Prince Charlie rose and it has an interesting history. It was first sent to Scotland from the garden of Charles Edward's villa in Rome as a present from the Prince to Mrs Burnett of Elrich in Aberdeenshire. The two original plants survived for well over a hundred years and it was a cutting from one of these which was presented to the Royal Family and which flourishes so successfully at

Balmoral. The flower itself is a large double white and of a peculiar square shape in contrast to the normal roundness of the rose. Altogether a most interesting specimen.

Also to the right of the front door and past the borders of sweet-smelling plants, is the Tower Garden which takes its name from the clock-tower which overlooks it. It consists of an immaculate lawn, surrounded by manicured yews and in which four beds have been cut for planting out with annuals like stocks or pentstemons. This is one of the gardens which is always at its best during the Royal visit.

If one turns to the left at the main doorway one comes to the formal rose gardens. It is worth noting on the way, the narrow beds of flowers planted right against the Castle walls and filled with sweet-smelling lavender broken by little beds of more colourful flowers beneath the windows. The rose garden is enclosed by a low yew hedge and filled with a splendid variety of polyanthas. A grass path divides the main rose garden from the sunken garden which was built for Queen Mary many years ago. Here are more beds of polyanthas surrounded by a mixed border of all the homely flowers – catmint and scabious, cornflower and antirrhinums, petunias and asters – a real riot of colour in the best Balmoral tradition and a welcome relief from the strictly regimented rose beds. The drystone wall which encloses the sunken garden has been planted up with all manner of Alpine plants from aubretias to mesembryanthemums which add to the overall effect of colour.

Another exceptionally colourful garden is the pansy garden which was the especial delight of George VI whose bedroom windows looked out over it. It is also overlooked by a terrace which the Royal Family often use in warm weather for out-of-door meals. Looking down on it when the pansies are in full bloom is to appreciate George VI's dictum that flower gardens should be all flowers. They carpet the beds completely so that there is hardly any earth to be seen. George VI and Queen Elizabeth were great landscapers. He laid down that his gardens should be designed to look their best when viewed from the windows of the house which is, after all, the way in which they are most commonly seen. Nor could he bear the aids so often used by enthusiastic gardeners such as pea sticks for supports. Everything had to look as natural as possible so, if the gardeners had to use any sort of props, they had to be most cunningly concealed.

At the far end of the great sweep of lawn which lies in front of the Castle is the area known as Queen Mary's Garden. There is a fountain in the centre and round it beds of flowers which vary with the seasons of the year. Beyond this, down some granite steps, is another oblong shaped garden featuring an herbaceous border and a giant gean tree. When Mr Shewell-Cooper, the great horticulturist, was shown around the Balmoral Gardens by George VI and Queen Elizabeth, his keen eye detected something odd about the great gean. Closer inspection disclosed that there was a gooseberry bush

Previous page:
Balmoral

Sunken pansy garden at Balmoral

Charles and Anne with one of the Queen's corgis
at the gamekeeper's cottage, Balmoral

A view of Birkhall and its steeply banked garden.
It is the present home of the Queen Mother

growing out of a hole in its trunk. As he remarks, it must be one of the few places where you can pick gooseberries off a cherry tree!

On the domestic side, the fruit and vegetable gardens are designed to supply the considerable needs of the Castle. The lush strawberry and raspberry crops have already been mentioned. There are also red currants and black currants, lettuces and tomatoes, potatoes, carrots and parsnips. Just the sort of things you would expect to find in an average country garden, although on a rather larger scale. The great difficulty with which the Royal gardeners have to contend is the late frosts which can strike as late as August and can be quite severe as Balmoral is over 1,000 feet above sea level. Just the same, as the time comes round each year for the Royal visit, everything contrives to be at its best to welcome them – a triumph for good husbandry and one which adds much pleasure to their stay.

Of the other Royal gardens in the north, those surrounding Abergeldie Castle are perhaps the best known. The old Elizabethan garden was allowed to grow rather wild during the war and much of it was put down to vegetables. It is now getting back to some of its former glory with its neat little box borders and fine flower beds. It is well worth a visit and is open to the public.

Sunken rock garden at
Balmoral

Birkhall

Three miles to the south west of Balmoral, nestling in a hollow of the forest, lies Birkhall, loveliest and most comfortable of all the Royal Homes. Significantly, the white-walled Jacobite house has been the setting for four royal honeymoons – those of the Queen, Princess Margaret, Princess Alexandra and the Duchess of Kent. 'It is the nicest place in the whole world' said a twelve-years-old Princess Elizabeth.

Birkhall – 'Bonnie Birka' – belongs to her mother, and is much more a family home than any of the palaces or castles. It is a small, superbly comfortable country house that requires the minimum of upkeep and servants, and affords the maximum privacy. Queen Victoria visited Florence Nightingale there, and was so delighted she immediately offered to buy it from the Gordon family, who had built it in 1715. Whether the Gordons were willing vendors is not known, but the Queen was a determined buyer, for the house solved a pressing problem for her: she gave it to the Prince of Wales (later Edward VII) so that he need not entertain his rowdy friends at Balmoral. 'See that the smoking room is closed at midnight' she had instructed the Master of the Household in the castle – and this order had brought a family crisis, only a few days before. Now, with Birkhall, he could take them all there and smoke all night, if he wanted to.

For such a small property there are immense grounds: thirty thousand acres, mostly rock and scree, but with three sizeable lochs and a salmon-rich river, the Muick. A mile or two away from the house, at the Falls of Muick, a new salmon-leap has been dynamited out of the rock, and is now one of the finest in Britain.

The Queen Mother first took a serious interest in Birkhall a few years after her marriage, and considered it a more suitable holiday home for her two daughters than Balmoral. She supervised every detail of decoration and furnishing and allowed no museum pieces to mar the effect of light, airy rooms designed especially for informality.

Ten years ago she enlarged the house, perhaps envisaging the more-frequent use it was about to receive by her growing family of grandchildren, nephews and nieces. To one wing she added four bedrooms and four bathrooms, and completely rebuilt the kitchen. Central heating and air conditioning were installed, and the electrical wiring renewed. Birkhall is so attractive that, while all this was going on, visitors still arrived and were content to live in caravans on the lawn!

A noticeable feature of the house is the lay-out of the gardens at the rear which, while seeming casual, was planned with painstaking care and advice from some of the finest landscape artists in Britain. Great banks of laburnum

Birkhall: the rear garden

shelter the lawns, and a sweeping curve of tulips, blood-red and four feet high, lead the eye down to the river bank below. Here, a tree has been removed to open up a view; there, a hedge growing carelessly wild, carefully concealing the sight of a road. 'It was made for a honeymoon' said the young Duchess of Kent, after spending hers there. And that is a tribute that could apply to only one of the royal homes. Birkhall.

The gardens at Birkhall, now the home of the Queen Mother, present special problems of their own. The vegetable garden for instance, although of splendidly rich loam soil, is on a steep slope of one in eight which makes it difficult to work, to say the least. It is, however, a very productive garden and much loved by the Queen Mother who calls it 'delicious'. There are flowers everywhere with little formality about their grouping. It is, in fact, like a cottage garden on a rather grander scale. One of its most unusual features is the herbaceous border on the west side of the house where the ground has been banked up to accommodate it. It must be singularly suitable soil for the clumps of perennials which grow there are of really remarkable size. By contrast the apple trees which make up a small orchard, planted by George VI and Queen Elizabeth, have never produced more than a few rather undersized apples – nobody knows why.

Perhaps, of all the Royal Gardens, Birkhall is the 'cosiest'. It wanders off in unexpected directions, there are odd summer houses dotted about and a general air of peace and restfulness which, for many people, is the most desirable property of a garden.

Queen Victoria had a positive passion for seclusion and it was this which led her to create the most remote of all the Royal residences. This was Alt-na-Guithasach which she had built in the wilds of Glen Muick far beyond Birkhall. It stands overlooking the often sinister waters of the loch and is surrounded on all sides by towering hills. The Queen usually referred to it as 'The Hut' or 'The Bothie' and indeed it is little more by Royal standards. It consists of two buildings of which the larger contains two sitting-rooms, a bedroom and dressing room and a small bedroom for a lady-in-waiting and another for a maid. The smaller building gives accommodation for the domestic staff. Here the Queen could really be 'away from it all'. She used it as a base for her long treks into the hills or spent the days picnicking by the loch or fishing. She so loved the nights that she spent there with the Prince that, after he died, she could never bear to sleep there again because of the memories it held. To the end of her life, however, she continued to visit it, and it has been used as a base for picnics and excursions by the Royal Family ever since.

Castle of Mey

Scottish castles have a mystique, a grandeur, that is happily unique. From afar: fairy-like; come closer, they are stern, forbidding; enter, they are mellow and warm. The better castles, that is; the ones which are lived in by people who love them. For castles need to be loved.

Barrogill, better known as the Castle of Mey, is a good example.

Not many years ago it lay discarded, old and ugly, glowering, it seemed, in sullen rebuke. It huddles defensively on the northernmost shore of the mainland, dominating nothing beyond a strip of beach and a mile or two of the rushing waters of the Pentland Firth. It was even overlooked by an ordinary house, perched on the heights of Dunnet Head. As a castle it was a failure; as a home it did not exist.

In the summer of 1952 the Queen Mother, recently a widow, saw Barrogill for the first time and resolved to bring it to life. The fourteen years since have seen a greater transformation than in the whole of its previous four centuries of history.

The first owner, the Fourth Earl of Caithness, went bankrupt building it; the Fifth Earl lived there for a time, disinterestedly, and from 1600 on it suffered almost continuous assaults, being plundered and burned with great regularity and receiving scars that were never completely repaired. The final indignity, that of being abandoned, came with the twentieth century Rating Acts, and it was when the roof was about to fall in, literally, that the Queen Mother arrived.

Using local builders and firing them with her own enthusiasm, she completed enough repairs to make the castle habitable in six months. When she returned to London, villagers would wander down the driveway to see what was going on, to return home perhaps hours later having shifted a pile of rubble, weeded a path or cleaned out a derelict greenhouse. Some, unknown to anyone, planted seeds in the once-overgrown garden.

Throughout 1953 the face-lift operation continued, with the Queen Mother flying to Wick from London or Aberdeen at every opportunity. While away she would have been studying photographs of each room, and back in Barrogill wasted no time in passing on her ideas.

Stone-flagged walls stayed, but had to be scrubbed; floors left as they were and levelled only if dangerous. Great areas were covered with coco-nut matting; the colour and texture blended with the stone and wood. Big walls and gloomy corridors were painted white. New fireplaces were installed, using the old stone; double-glazed windows blocked the northern draughts, and useless chimneys were filled in. Mould, damp patches, even echoes, disappeared. A grim, grey room in the tower became a boudoir, with white

The prolific garden of the Castle of Mey

walls, red velvet curtains and chintzy furniture; an even uglier room became a glossy modern bathroom. Exterior woodwork – window and door-frames – were picked out with bright white paint, and suddenly Barrogill seemed to be alive again.

The gardens had also been under close scrutiny, but here the new owner's plan was to restore them exactly as they had always been. Lawns, with thick, springy turf, stretch away on the western side, protected by a wind-break of trees and holly-bushes. On the east there are two large walled gardens for flowers and vegetables, the flowering beds laid out formally with wide divisions of crazy paving. Creepers cover most of the ten-foot-high surrounding walls.

Vegetables flourish happily, but many of the commoner varieties of flowers, dahlias for example, do not take kindly to the spartan conditions of Caithness. Large greenhouses, however, supply indoor decoration all the year. Local gardeners say that they did not realise what could be grown and what could survive in the area until they saw what was coming up in the grounds of Barrogill. In fact, they look at the castle with new respect and a little pride now; everyone is a little happier. Even, perhaps, the castle.

The Queen Mother's drawing room at the Castle of Mey

Holyroodhouse

The Palace of Holyrood, outside Edinburgh, is the official home of the Royal Family when in Scotland. In function it may be said to be the Buckingham Palace of the north, but, in historical interest, it is the rival to Windsor.

The origins of Holyrood, like so many of Scotland's ancient houses, is steeped in legend. It is said that while David I, King of the Scots, was out hunting he was attacked by a stag which wounded him in the leg. To defend himself, he siezed the stag's antlers. In an instant the stag disappeared and he found himself grasping a cross instead. That night he dreamed that a voice told him to 'make a house for the Canons devoted to the Cross'. Thus he came to found the Augustine Abbey of Holyrood at the place where the struggle with the stag had occurred. The Abbey was founded in 1128 and linked to the township of Edinburgh by a road appropriately known as Canongate. Today, Holyroodhouse looks out on one side over the still open land of Salisbury Crag which, at its highest point, is known as Arthur's Seat and, on the other side, the City of Edinburgh crowds against the Palace walls.

After its foundation, Holyrood continued as a religious establishment for over four hundred years. Its importance is demonstrated by the fact that Royalty frequently stayed there but it was in no way a Royal residence. The monks went about their quiet business, tilling the ground around the Abbey and offering hospitality to the wayfarer. Its peculiarly close relationship with Royalty may be judged, however, by the example set by James II. He was born there, crowned there, married there and is buried there. Finally James IV decided to build a palace there. He was killed at Flodden before it could be completed but his son James V carried on the work. When it was completed it must have been one of the finest houses in Scotland but it was not to survive for very long. In 1544 it was sacked by the English and set fire to. In the resulting conflagration the already ancient Abbey was also destroyed which must be counted as almost as great a tragedy as if Westminster Abbey had been destroyed at some stage in its history.

Scarcely twenty years after this disaster, the Palace buildings had been sufficiently restored to make a home for Mary, Queen of Scots, but all that remained of the original building was the north west tower. She took possession in 1561 and spent some of the happiest years of her tragic life there. Contemporary drawings show it to have been a modestly imposing residence of which one of the most charming features was the pleasure gardens. They consisted of a series of small gardens opening out of one another with attractive glades and bowers, the whole being enclosed by a high, beautifully trimmed hedge. In 1565 she married Lord Darnley there and so set in train the tragic events which were to darken her life. It was at Holyrood, a year later, that Rizzio was murdered at her feet. By the next year Darnley had

Holyrood

himself been murdered and the Queen had married Bothwell. Three weeks later she left Holyrood for the last time.

The Palace lay empty for twenty years until James VI re-established his Court there in 1578. It remained there for a quarter of a century until James succeeded also to the English throne. From that day on the Palace has only been lived in by British Sovereigns for short periods.

Its relative unimportance as a Royal residence did not, however, save it from the crusading zeal of Cromwell's soldiers at whose hands it suffered a second destruction. In 1671, on the restoration of the Monarchy, Charles II had the Palace rebuilt. The result is the classic Palace which we know today but it seems to lack the feeling of a house built as a home and added to by succeeding generations out of love. There are fine rooms and a certain majesty about the place but the criticism remains.

In 1745 Holyrood Palace had again its moment of glory. A few days after routing General Cope's army at Prestonpans, Bonnie Prince Charlie led his Highlanders in triumph through Edinburgh and, in the evening, gave a glittering State Ball at Holyrood. It was an event which is remembered with great nostalgia in Scotland but it was only a brief flicker of the flame. In the long years which followed the failure of the '45 Rebellion, the Palace again lay empty and deserted. After the French Revolution, George III allowed the Comte d'Artois to use it as his residence but it was not until 1822 that it was to entertain Royalty again. In that year George IV became the first Monarch to enter Holyrood since Charles I. He stayed there a fortnight and delighted the Scots (and amused them) by dressing in a kilt. He also gave a great banquet in his Palace before returning to London and drank toasts to the Chieftains and Clans of Scotland in the native whisky.

Holyrood had to wait another twenty years before Queen Victoria travelled north by which time the State Apartments had become quite uninhabitable. Just the same she found it 'a princely and most beautiful place' and gave orders that it was to be put into a proper state of repair. It is perhaps only a pity that the gardens should have attracted the attention of the Prince Consort with his love of the practical and orderly. He drew up new plans for the gardens in 1857 and, when they were implemented, the last link with the past was swept away. He had the little plantations and sheltered nooks, so beloved by Mary Queen of Scots and her courtiers, completely removed. In their place he had laid out a rectangular plot of about sixteen acres. Divided into the North Garden and the South Garden by the new east wing extension of the Palace, they are remarkable only for their symmetry and precise design. There are no sheltering walls or hedges, so that the whole plan can be seen at a glance and the impression gained is more of public gardens than anything else. Only one relic of the past has been retained. This is an old sundial which was made by John Mylne in 1633 at the time of the rebuilding by Charles II and which stands in the North Garden near the north west tower.

The Braemar Games is an annual event seldom missed by the Royal Family

Just the same, Holyroodhouse cannot entirely escape from the romance of its history. It does not need a great imagination to hear the whisper of its ghosts and, if reminder is needed, there are the fine views to the south and east of the country over which David I hunted the stag and, closer to, the ruins of the Abbey which he founded.

Some of the glory, too, has returned. It is at Holyroodhouse that the Queen stays when she opens the Scottish social season with the Royal Garden parties and some of the old ceremonies have been revived. To see her there, surrounded by her Royal Company of Archers, dressed in their traditional uniform, is to take a step back into history when Holyrood Palace and the Abbey had their finest hour.

Off on holiday to Balmoral: the Royal Train
leaves Euston

The Royal Trains

It is said that the Queen prefers trains to all other methods of transport, but she uses them less than her great-grandmother, or even her father. The Royal Train is, in fact, no longer the splendid ten-coach palace-on-wheels of Queen Victoria's day, and has been reduced to two permanent coaches to which others are added from normal rolling-stock when necessary.

These two are kept at Wolverton, Buckinghamshire, and though they seldom carry the Queen, they have to be in a constant state of readiness for use if bad weather prevents take-off by the Queen's Flight. Modernisation of the railways in Britain has cut the Royal Train journeys by half, for both the stations at Ballater (for Balmoral) and Sandringham were scheduled for closure under the Beeching plan.

Nevertheless, there is a dignity and splendour attached to the train which can never be matched by cars or aeroplanes. The arrival of the Queen at the great stations of Euston, Edinburgh, Perth or Glasgow are truly royal occasions, and the gleaming, chocolate-brown coaches revealing, through huge, shiny windows, a glimpse of the regal opulence within, form a fitting backcloth to a monarch's progress. It must be said now that the days of the Royal train are numbered; it is unlikely to outlast the seventies.

Queen Victoria's train was, understandably, magnificent. It is said that seventy men were employed in cleaning and maintaining it, after the style of painting the Forth bridge. There were huge overstuffed chairs and settees; day-rooms, retiring-rooms, recreation rooms were all furnished as in a rather cramped palace, with bric-a-brac and aspidistras everywhere. The length of the train was a minor consideration, and depended only on the amount of baggage being taken; if there were too many coaches for one engine, then another engine was attached. And just as today's royal planes have a 'Purple Airway' cleared for them, so did Queen Victoria's train. All other trains for an hour in front were shunted off the line, and Her Majesty was carried from A to B non-stop, at speeds often equalling those of British Rail's crack expresses.

King Edward and King George V maintained the tradition of the ceremonial train but removed the heavier Victoriana and the forest of aspidistras. It was not re-designed completely, however, until King George VI arrived, and then the exigencies of war brought such unwelcome features as a bullet-proof box-car and blacked-out windows, and the sixteen coats of glossy paint were smothered in ugly camouflage.

The Royal Train was several times the target of German bombs, but it emerged comparatively unscathed, though it had taken the King all over Britain to visit the worst-hit cities and towns. King George, like his eldest

The pre-war Royal Train, with some pieces taken
from Queen Victoria's train. This was the Queen's
day saloon

Predecessor to the present Royal Train: George VI's office. This was the last of the Royal Trains; today there are only two coaches

daughter, was fond of trains, and it must have been a memorable experience for him to have used the specially-built train provided by the South African Government for his tour there immediately after the war. It was, said the experts, the finest train ever built, completely equipped with everything from full-size bathrooms, to telephones and air-conditioning.

In Britain there was a shortage of new rolling-stock, and plans for a new Royal Train were to be shelved for nearly ten years. Even the improvements that were made to the old coaches were somewhat utilitarian in appearance. When Elizabeth became Queen, it soon became apparent that her pattern of travel would be completely different to that of her father: long journeys by fast car, longer journeys by plane. The train was relegated to the task of

The Queen and Princess Anne are greeted on their return from Scotland

carrying her to Sandringham and Balmoral on holiday – and then chiefly because of its unlimited baggage capacity.

So the new train, when it was finally built, was miniature compared to its predecessors. Nevertheless, it is a masterpiece of ingenuity and tasteful decoration. The Queen's day-coach is similar to the interior of an aircraft, with light modern furniture and pastel colours. Prince Philip has installed an office, and a switchboard can connect him to any of the staff on the train or, through a scrambler device, to the GPO lines at a station. Kitchens, too, are like aircraft galleys, though the food is not pre-cooked; Royal train chefs take tremendous pride in their ability to produce six-course meals that would not disgrace a five-star hotel.

The two permanent coaches are specially-insulated against noise, and specially sprung. Here again, as with the royal aircraft, Prince Philip took a personal interest in the design and use of the most modern materials, but he is noticeably less fond of the train than the Queen. Ironically, the train staff at Wolverton have on several occasions seen him passing overhead – in his helicopter!

Saloon on the Royal Train

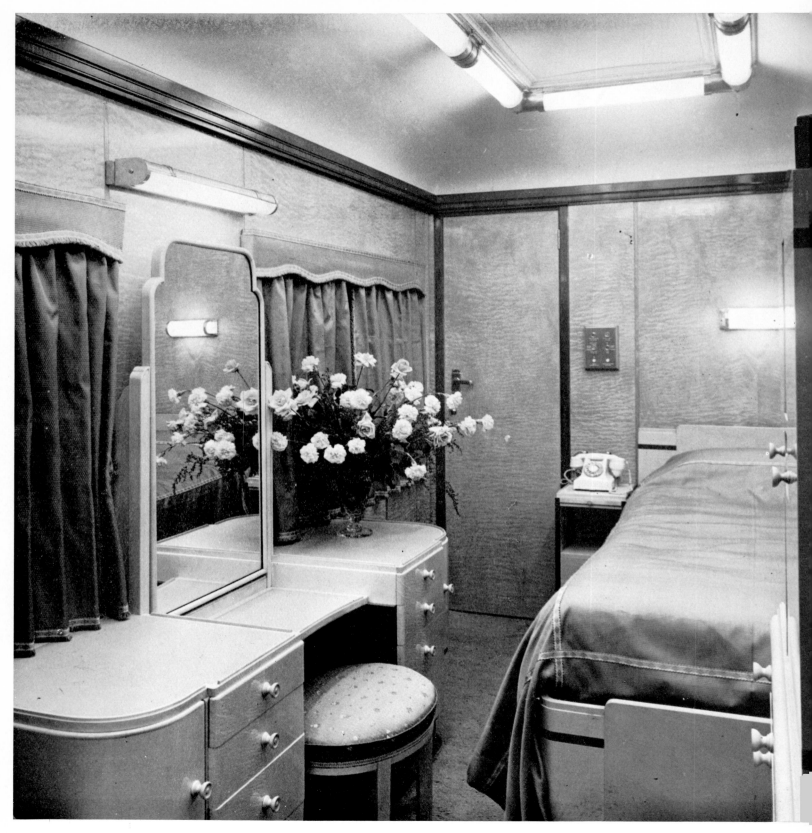

Left:
The Queen's bedroom on the specially-built train used for the Royal Tour of South Africa in 1947

Right:
George VI's Royal Train. During the war it covered 36,000 miles. Mr Tyles, the King's personal attendant, lays the table in the Royal Dining Car

Prince Philip is both pilot and passenger. He flies all types of Queen's Flight aircraft

The Queen's Flight

When King George V first set foot inside an aeroplane, it was not only an historic moment, but a perilous one, according to his advisers. None of them wanted the responsibility of encouraging His Majesty to fly, and it was only his own insistence, and his pride in the Royal Air Force, that allowed him to become airborne. The plane was a little Airspeed Envoy; the flight went without a hitch; King George is said to have enjoyed it greatly; and the Royal Flight – the King's Flight – was born.

Trophies from those days are still jealously guarded at the huge Transport Command base at Benson, Oxfordshire, where the Flight today occupies a special hanger and administrative headquarters. King George had a grass runway, four mechanics and one plane made of plywood and fabric. Today one hundred RAF men service two turbo-prop Andovers, two Whirlwind helicopters equipped with floats and a Chipmunk trainer. They are all constantly in use, carrying members of the Royal Family all over Britain, or on loan to Ministers or foreign guests, or delivering State papers. Royal flights average fifteen a month, and with the stringent servicing that keeps half the flight grounded in rotation there would need to be more aircraft were it not for the Comets and Boeings that are loaned from the RAF and BOAC.

The Queen had probably her first taste of flying in far-from-comfortable circumstances: during mock emergencies in the 1940s. An American Liberator, painted black, without markings except for the RAF roundels, was stationed at Farnborough, Hampshire, on a twenty-four-hour standby. Its sole purpose was to evacuate the Royal Family in the event of invasion. Its destination was to be Canada.

Every day a flight plan was made out; every day special weather reports obtained and liason established with the fighter wing whose job it would be to escort the plane to its first stop, Northern Ireland. Happily, that Royal Flight was never used in earnest, but to keep the crews alert several full-scale rehearsals were held, with the King, Queen and the two Princesses brought by car from Buckingham Palace or Windsor. They would climb into the cold, sparsely-furnished interior of the Liberator with a minimum amount of luggage, practice dinghy drill, then take off for a half-hour's circuit of the airfield. King George complained bitterly about these rehearsals, insisting that if the worst happened to Britain he would refuse to leave, anyway.

The Queen's planes today are a far cry from that cramped, ill-lit Liberator; the two Andovers (Avro 748s) are among the most luxurious in the air, for their size. They joined the flight in 1964, taking the place of less-powerful and less-adaptable Herons, for medium-range flights in the UK and Europe.

As a commercial plane the Andover seats sixty, but the Royal planes carry a maximum of twenty.

The interiors were designed by Gaby Schreiber from suggestions by the Queen and Prince Philip. There are two cabins, both decorated in blue, grey and yellow. The Queen's personal cabin is at the rear, with two swivelling seats and a settee converting into a divan bed. The forward cabin is divided into two sections, each with eight seats and large luggage compartments, and a small changing-room for the Queen and her husband.

The exteriors of the planes were until recently painted red, but this was stripped off when pilots complained that the heavy fluorescent paint was hampering control surfaces and making the aircraft clumsy to handle. Today fuselages are predominantly polished metal. Pilots and ground crew are all men of exceptional ability, and appointment to the Queen's Flight is a rare honour. The present commander is Air Commodore John H. L. Blount, DFC. He is responsible for all the Queen's flying arrangements, including world tours when a Boeing 707 may have to be chartered from BOAC. Transport Command have a much-used Comet with long-range fuel tanks for VIP travel, and both the Queen and Prince Philip have used this on several occasions. It is on this plane that the only WRAF personnel in the service are used – as stewardesses.

All Queen's Flight aircraft have priority from air traffic controllers over Britain, and if they carry royal passengers, priority anywhere in the West. A corridor of free airspace known as the 'Purple Airway' is established well ahead of them, ten miles wide and four thousand feet deep. All pilots are banned from using this corridor from half an hour before the royal plane passes until half an hour afterwards. Controllers estimate that just one flight takes twenty-four hours continuous work to arrange a path through the crowded airways – something that King George V, in his Airspeed Envoy, could never have envisaged.

Herons of the Queen's Flight

A Whirlwind helicopter, newest addition to the Queen's Flight. Prince Philip is a qualified pilot

Ante-room and drawing room

Britannia

From the days of Cleopatra, Royal ships have held an aura of romance and mystery. But while smaller countries with fewer maritime connections have had a long history of Royal and Presidential yachts, it was not until Victoria's reign that Britain's Head of State possessed one.

The *Victoria and Albert*, however, was by no means a sea-going vessel in the strict sense; it was more of a floating annexe to Osborne. Much of the furniture was heavy both physically and aesthetically; the Queen liked to be surrounded by familiar objects, and if they included huge and impractical overstuffed suites and ornately-carved tables, then they were loaded on to the protesting structure of the *V and A*, as it was known. The Queen was a good sailor, and enjoyed rough weather, but the ship did not. It is reported that it creaked alarmingly, and at one time or another most of Her Majesty's ministers (and a great many foreign potentates too) were sick on board. Its most frequent use was for carrying the Queen and her suite up and down the lines of warships at the Spithead Review, and for dispensing hospitality during Cowes Week.

There is little in common between the *V and A* and today's Royal Yacht *Britannia*. *Britannia* was originally the idea of King George VI, but plans were scrapped at the outbreak of war. In 1948 the Admiralty re-embarked on the project, and it was decided that the ship should fill a dual role – that of Royal home and (in wartime) a hospital ship. Every detail of construction was planned with this in mind, and if necessary its conversion could take place within three months.

The *Britannia* is one of the most modern ships afloat, and even though it was originally launched thirteen years ago, it has been constantly overhauled and its equipment improved to keep the ship one step ahead of its time in safety, usefulness and comfort.

It has travelled around the world several times, from Canada to New Zealand, and has been used for every kind of Royal function, from honeymoons to extensive Royal tours and such festivities as Independence Day celebrations of Commonwealth countries. Prince Philip, needless to say, has used the yacht extensively to experiment with new types of naval equipment. Though primarily a Royal home, it is very much a workshop, showcase and transporter, too.

Britannia cost £2,000,000 to build. It is 412 feet in length and 55 feet at its broadest. Displacement without stores is 3,990 tons, with stores (including 120 tons of water) 4,715 tons. Gross tonnage is 5,769 tons. Its engines develop 12,000 shp, with a maximum speed of 23 knots. There are 220 ratings and 22 officers in the normal complement.

The Queen's private drawing room on *Britannia*

Prince Philip's private study on *Britannia*. On the
wall: his old command, HMS *Magpie*

The drawing room

The *Britannia*'s dining room

One of the Royal ante-rooms on *Britannia*

Accommodation for the Royal Family is aft. The Queen's apartments are on the shelter deck between the masts, with a verandah at the after end leading to a sun deck. The main staircase from the Royal quarters leads to a vestibule on the upper deck, where the State apartments are found. Dining room, drawing room and ante-room extend the full width of the vessel without obstruction from pillars. Household and guest cabins, fitted out to first-class passenger liner standards, are on the main deck near the entrance ports. Royal staff are on the lower deck. There is a swimming pool, and the dining room can be instantly converted into a cinema. The ship is air-conditioned and stabilised.

The *Britannia*, with its label of being 'the most expensive ship afloat', has inevitably been the centre of a great deal of controversy since its launching. A number of MPs and newspaper columnists have conducted a sometimes bitter campaign against the expenditure which has been necessary to maintain its high standard of efficiency and availability. There have been suggestions that the ship should be used as an export-drive 'shop window', carrying British goods round the world, and a Labour MP asked the House to consider using it as an exhibition hall for the Crown Jewels!

The Admiralty have always flatly denied charges of extravagance: the new propellors, for example, which were fitted at a cost of £20,000, were the result of secret research into the problem of detection by submarine. The special blades were designed to produce the least possible noise and vibration; the Royal Yacht was chosen to test them out.

Britannia's officers resent such accusations because, they say, it is now virtually impossible to bring the accommodation for ratings up to the standard of a new warship without there being demands for committees of inquiry. Far from extravagances, they say, there have had to be the most rigorous economies.

It is interesting to note that, while there were no criticisms of the money spent on the *Victoria and Albert* when it was built, there were far greater grounds for complaint. By a farcical mistake, one of the designers confused metric tons (2,000 lb) with English tons (2,240 lb). The result was that the ship was grossly top-heavy, and would certainly have capsized. Unfortunately the error was only discovered when the ship was almost completed, and tremendous surgical operations had to be performed. The tall smokestacks were ruthlessly cut down, and the top deck removed. When possible, heavy machinery was moved to below the water-line, and many of the ornate fittings were taken out altogether. Water-tank tests showed the yacht was still unseaworthy, and it was only when 600 tons of concrete ballast was poured in that the *V and A* would float safely upright.

As with the *Britannia*, the actual expenditure vastly exceeded the estimates, but, as with the *Britannia*, the *V and A* produced an incalculable return in prestige. After its unhappy birth, Queen Victoria's floating palace gave many

Her Majesty's Yacht Britannia:
*A diagrammatic drawing showing the internal
lay-out of the yacht, which can be
converted to a hospital ship in time of war.*

Key to H.M. Yacht *Britannia*

Bridge, Shelter and Upper Decks:

1. Ensign Staff.
2. Anchor Light.
3. Quarterdeck.
4. Drawing-room.
5. Ante-room.
6. Sun Deck.
7. Mizzen Mast.
8. Verandah.
9. Royal Corridor.
10. Lift Shaft.
11 and 12. Royal Guests' Bedrooms and Bathrooms.
13 and 14. Maids' Rooms.
15 and 15A. Wardrobe Rooms.
16. Pantry, etc.
17. Queen's Bathroom.
18. Queen's Bedroom.
19. Duke of Edinburgh's Bedroom.
20. Duke of Edinburgh's Bathroom.
21. Queen's Sitting-Room.
22. Dining Room.
23. Servery and Scullery.
24. Valets' Bedrooms.
25. Mainmast.
26. 35-ft. Motor-boat (port).
27. Dinghy (stowed on deck).
28. Casing.
29. Royal Barge (starboard).
30. Dinghy (starboard).
31. 32-ft. Motor Cutter (starboard).
32. Motor Dinghy (starboard).
33. Fan Casing.
34. 35-ft. Motor-Boat (port).
35. Motor Dinghy (port).
36. 27-ft. Motor Sea Boat (starboard).
37. 27-ft. Motor Sea Boat (port).
38. Whip Aerials.
39. Foremast.
40. Radar Scanner.
41. Compass Platform.
42. Wing Bridge.
43. Officers' Sea Quarters.
44. Position of Officers' Galley.
45. Position of Ward Room.
46. Position of Officers' Cabins.
47. Position of Royal Chart House.
48. Accommodation Ladder (stowed).
49. Anchor Cables and Capstans.
50. Jackstaff.

Main Deck:

51. Staff Cabins.
52. Royal Household Cabins.
53. Lady Guests' Cabins.
54. Gentlemen of the Royal Household Smoking Room.
55. Cloakroom.
56. Lower Entrance.
57. Suite consisting of Sitting-Room and two Bedrooms.
58. Cabins.
59. Maids' Sitting-Room.
60. Air-conditioning Plant.
61. Medical Officers' Consulting Room.
62. Sick Bay and Operating Theatre.
63. Bathrooms.
64. Laundry.
65. C.P.O.s' Cabins.
66. P.O.s' Recreation Space.
67. Store.
68. Shipwright's Workshop.

Lower Deck:

69 and 69A. Staff Cabins.
70. Royal Clerks' Office.
71. Clerks' Office.
72. Main Turbine Engine Rooms.
73. Boiler Rooms.
74. Showers.
75. Seamen's Mess.
75A. Stokers' Mess.
76. Recreation Space.

Platform Deck:

77. Baggage Rooms.
78. Linen Stores.
79. Blanket Stores.
80. Wine Stores.
81. China Stores.
82. Auxiliary Machine Room.
83. Stabiliser Compartment and Starboard Stabiliser (inboard).
84. Engineers' Workshop.
85. Cold Rooms.
86. Store Rooms.
87. Starboard Propeller.
88. Fuel Tanks, etc.
89. Starboard Bilge Keel.
90. Waterline.

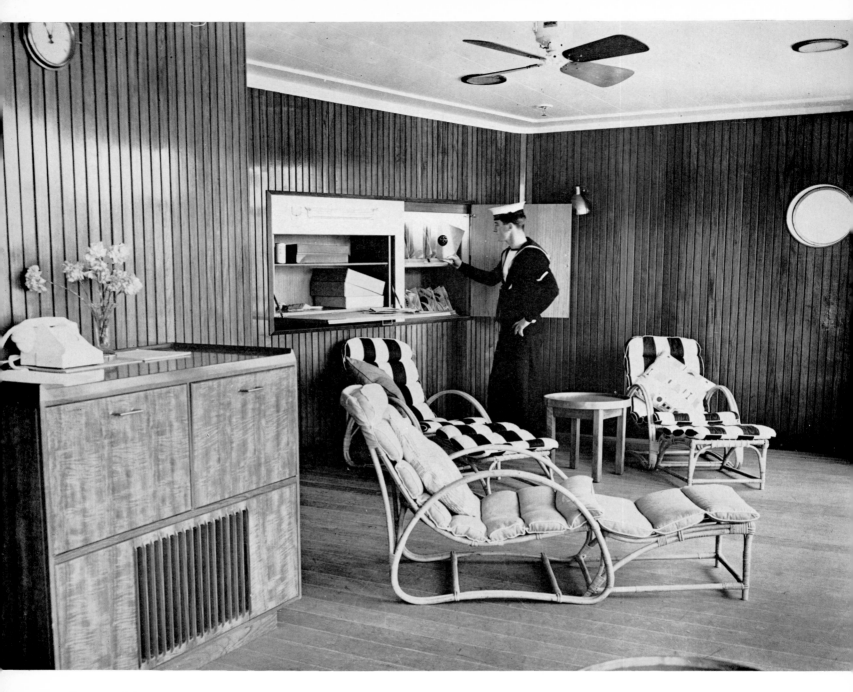

The verandah sun room on *Britannia*

years of service, and it was not until 1946 that the Admiralty finally pronounced it unsafe. It was broken up in 1955 and much of the furniture and fittings taken to Buckingham Palace.

King Edward VII was responsible for the uniforms that the Royal Yacht crews wear. While Royal Navy sailors have worn serge since the First World War, the *V and A* crews wore, and *Britannia* crews still wear, cloth trousers, specially made. The King, it is said, hated change. The Royal Marines on board have distinctive dress, too: on their right shoulders they wear white flashes, and, in tropical waters, they change into white drill with pointed-toe boots. On the upper deck, the crew work bare-headed, an odd tradition that is hard to trace back to its origin. One theory is that it dates from the days when sailors wore straw hats, easily lost overboard in strong winds. Another feature of life in the Royal Yacht is that of firing a gun twice a day, at 7 am and 9 pm. Queen Alexandra, on the *V and A*, set off the evening gun herself. And when the present Queen leaves the ship in the Royal barge, it is crewed by petty officers who have to change into the uniforms of ordinary seamen – again, for no readily apparent reason.

The barge, incidentally, would have disappointed Cleopatra, whose own barge, 'like a burnished throne, burned on the water'. The one carried by *Britannia* is 41 feet long, with two 120 hp diesels, and the only concession to luxury is in the upholstered leather seats.

Bloodhound

One of King Edward VII's closest friends was Thomas Lipton, the founder of the grocery chain, and one of their mutual interests was sailing. Lipton spent hundreds of thousands of pounds on the sport and, in particular, building a series of challengers for the America's Cup. His services to sailing were immeasurable, yet not even his friend the King could break down the snobbery of the Royal Yacht Squadron, who refused to let him in as a member until shortly before his death, when he had become Sir Thomas Lipton.

Today, the harbours of Cowes, Hamble and Poole are classless; Prince Philip competes with grocers, naval ratings, bankers and lawyers, and the Royal Yacht Squadron's snobbery is dead. Prince Philip sets an example by lending his own yacht, *Bloodhound*, to boys' clubs and sailing clubs for training, a gesture the more remarkable since *Bloodhound* is one of the finest racing yachts in Britain.

He bought her for £10,000 in January 1962 from Mr Myles Wyatt, chairman of British United Airways. She had sailed more than fifty-thousand ocean miles, and in 1952 came second in the Bermuda race – the only British entry ever to have done so well.

Bloodhound weighs thirty-four tons, has a waterline length of forty-five feet and an overall length of sixty-three feet. She was built in 1936 by Camper and Nicholson at Gosport, and designed by Charles Nicholson. Her first big victory was the Fastnet race in 1939 – the toughest yacht race in the world.

Prince Philip races frequently, with yachtsman-designer Uffa Fox, and taught Prince Charles and Princess Anne to sail in her. *Bloodhound* requires a minimum crew of eleven.

The previous Royal racing yacht was *Bluebottle*, Dragon Class, which on her retirement was presented to the Royal Naval College, Dartmouth. She was originally given to the Queen and Prince Philip as a wedding present by the Isle of Wight Island Sailing Club.

Prince Philip, Prince Charles
and Uffa Fox during Cowes
Regatta

Prince Philip with Princess Anne on board *Blood-hound* during the Britannia Challenge Cup Race at Cowes

Prince Charles and Princess
Anne collect fresh water
supplies for *Bloodhound* at
Fanagmore, Sutherland

Acknowledgements

The authors gratefully acknowledge the co-operation of the following in granting permission for the reproduction of the illustrations contained in this book:

The Lord Chamberlain; The Ministry of Defence; J Allan Cash, FIBP, FRPS; J E Downward, FIBP; Albert W Kerr, FIBP, FRPS; Ray Bellisario; Fox Photos; LEA; Studio Lisa; Fleetway Publications; Syndication International; Horticultural Photo Supply Service; The British Travel Association; Keystone Press; Orbit Press; Central Press; Press Association; Topix; Camera Press; *Daily Express*; *The Times*; *Country Life*; *Woman's Journal*; and the *Radio Times* Hulton Picture Library.

Bibliography

Thatched with Gold *by Lady Airlie*. Hutchinson

Sandringham *by Helen Cathcart*. W H Allen.

Balmoral *by Ivor Brown*. Collins.

The Royal Residences of Great Britain *by Neville Williams*. Barrie & Rockliff.

Lady Lytton's Court Diary *Ed Mary Lutyens*. Hart-Davis.

The History and Treasures of Windsor Castle *by B J W Hill* MA. Pitkin Pictorials Ltd.

Buckingham Palace *by Marguerite D Peacock*. Pitkin Pictorials Ltd.

The Royal Mews Official Guide. Pitkin Pictorials Ltd.

Royal Gardens *by Lanning Roper*. W H & L Collingridge Ltd.

The Royal Gardeners *by W E Shewell-Cooper*. Cassell & Co Ltd.